D0860113

"WE OR THEY"

THE MACMILLAN COMPANY
NEW YORK · BOSTON · CHICAGO · DALLAS
ATLANTA · SAN FRANCISCO

MACMILLAN & CO., Limited
LONDON · BOMBAY · CALCUTTA
MELBOURNE

THE MACMILLAN COMPANY
OF CANADA, Limited
TORONTO

"WE OR THEY"

TWO WORLDS IN CONFLICT

By

HAMILTON FISH ARMSTRONG

◆

NEW YORK

THE MACMILLAN COMPANY

1937

Copyright, 1936, by
THE MACMILLAN COMPANY.

All rights reserved—no part of this book
may be reproduced in any form without
permission in writing from the publisher,
except by a reviewer who wishes to quote brief
passages in connection with a review written
for inclusion in magazine or newspaper.

Reprinted January, 1937; February, 1937 (three times);
March, 1937.

PRINTED IN THE UNITED STATES OF AMERICA
BY THE STRATFORD PRESS, INC., NEW YORK

Libr…
I.U.P.
Indiana, Pa.

321.4 Ar57w
c. 1

To Those Honorable Men
in Prison and in Exile
for Liberty

CONTENTS

"WE OR THEY"

I.

TWO WORLDS

To thee, old cause!
Thou peerless, passionate, good cause,
Thou stern, remorseless, sweet idea,
Deathless throughout the ages, races, lands.
—*Walt Whitman*

OTHER Americans have like myself listened to League debates, compact of declarations, appeals, warnings, reservations; have talked with elected leaders in the capitals and corners of Europe—thousands of them, literally, in these eighteen years—some perfunctory and pompous, some cynical and witty, some bombastic and tearful, some dignified, a few generous, two or three prescient and serene; have watched elections and plebiscites, café riots and strikes; have sat on countless iron chairs on countless terraces reading the conflicting reports of countless cabinet crises; have seen kings wade in trout streams, kneel rigid at midnight mass, open parliaments, lie in state; have watched so many kinds of men march—shouting or grim, desperate for bread, entranced by a slogan, on fire for a leader, in delirium for freedom won, in relief for freedom lost; have had private exhibitions of this dictator's magnetic eye and squared shoulders, special auditions of that one's wet and crescendo

speech, as showy as a skyrocket and as convincing;
have heard amplifiers blare and crowds thunder—
Piazza Venezia, Red Square, Pariser-platz, Puerta
del Sol, Ringstrasse—windows shuttered in fear or
cascading flags and carpets and flowers; have hud-
dled in attics with ex-Premiers around a gas-ring
and a plate of speckled cakes; have seen wreaths
fade on monuments and barbed wire rust in the
undergrowth by quiet streams and chimneys smoke
where new guns and gases are made.

Nobody who has watched this confusion of
struggling men and systems can have refrained
from speculating on the relative merits of democracy and dictatorship. In the United States the
choice is made—made by reason and instinct. Most
Americans, ranking governments by their ability
to afford the greatest number the greatest material
good, still consider democracy best able to do this,
and without the spiritual sacrifice which the dictators exact. And there still are many who would
prefer, in Newton Baker's words, "to be poor if
necessary, but in any case free." But there is another question. Can tolerably satisfactory relations
ever in fact be established between peoples free
and peoples in chains? Is not the gulf too wide?
As the tide of violence rushes on from one vortex
to another—the invasion of Manchuria, the murder of Dollfuss, the scrapping of Locarno, the fall of
Addis Ababa, Fascist planes over Madrid—the question takes more acute form. Even if tolerable relations ever are somehow established, can they last
for long? Is not the gulf too deep?

II.

THE GULF BETWEEN

The people are converted into fuel to feed the mere machine which is the State. The skeleton eats up the flesh around it. The scaffolding becomes the owner and tenant of the house.
—José Ortega y Gasset

THE gulf between the two conceptions of life is indeed deep and wide. Here, not absolute freedom certainly but great and precious freedom—freedom to think, to believe, to disbelieve, to speak, to will, to choose. There, not some freedom, but none— nothing but obeisance, body, mind and soul, before the iron will and upstretched arm of a restless, infallible master. But what makes us speculate so somberly on the possibility of maintaining tolerable relations between these two worlds is not just that the dictators and their entourage of made-to-order philosophers, bogus scientists, subservient courts and dictated press hold different conceptions from ours about everything which we consider of importance. After revising histories, philosophies, bibles and law codes they have proceeded to a revision of the dictionary itself. As a result, intercommunication across the abyss has become almost impossible. And with all means of argument, explanation and accommodation swept away, there grows up on both sides a not unjustifiable

3

belief in the inevitability of a prolonged struggle
for supremacy and survival.

The lines are drawn in terms both general and
specific. On the one side are nations which assume
that human beings have individual minds, wills and
aspirations, and that this is the fact which differen-
tiates them from other animals; that they have ca-
pacities for self-improvement, even if very slowly;
and that they should be allowed to use their minds,
exercise their wills, and manage their own affairs
as a means of learning how to do all these things
better. Obviously the governments of these democratic nations are not ideal. They shelter plenty of
narrow and selfish individuals who mistrust popular education and fear the power of the masses. But
to the extent that these influence policy they must
circumvent law and enlightened public opinion.

On the other side are nations which have never
fully accepted the democratic conception of human
progress, or which have discarded it because that
sort of progress is aggravatingly slow and undra-
matic. The people in these states are living according to the rules of definitive systems revealed to
infallible men or groups of men, imposed and
enforced by decrees and bullets, and considered
permanently immune to criticism, first because infallible men do not need criticism, secondly—and
more simply—because they will not tolerate it. To
us, these nations are now so far away that they
seem on different planets. Those planets revolve
around different suns from the ones we know.
Each sun is a man—only a man—subject to the

weaknesses, bodily and mental and moral, of other men. But he is set up on high where his aberrations affect the comfort, security and even the lives of millions of other men and women. A great number of these may mistrust or hate him. But their opinions and supplications do not carry through the thin cold air of his lofty altitudes, and they have no means to protect themselves from his possible folly. They are trapped.

Of course this is not a new phenomenon. But each time it happens those who are caught in the trap are astonished. The members of the legislative assembly of the Second Republic voted in 1849 the law which enabled Napoleon III to achieve his coup d'état. They kept on good terms with him while he cleared the administration of republicans, censored the press and suppressed the right of meetings. Then he calmly utilized the same law to put them in prison. Lessons like these carried no warning to the liberal parties in Italy which thought to make use of Fascism just long enough to suppress their Socialist rivals, nor to the Italian industrialists who welcomed the Fascist solution of the labor problem on the erroneous assumption that the embryo dictator would remain "their man," that he would not inevitably swallow up the interests of both employer and employee in the interest of his personal régime. Neither did historical precedent warn earnest Germans like Brüning that once they had circumvented constitutional safeguards even in what seemed a good cause, once they had shown how to govern without Parliament

by a system of exceptional laws and decrees, the
stage would be set for the von Schleichers and von
Papens, with the Hitlers and Goerings close on
their heels. The von Papens and von Schleichers
themselves were equally erroneous in imagining
that they could make electoral bargains with people like the Nazis and still continue themselves to
be the dominant factor in a system which had the
pretense of being parliamentary. They all learnt
too late that once a dictator has been permitted to
entrench himself behind the guns and money bags
of the state, and to monopolize the springs of public information and opinion, there remains for
everyone else a very limited choice of alternatives.
They may crowd abjectly about the steps of the
new throne. Or they may conspire underground,
at the risk of their lives. Or they may utter individual protests, and be put in jail. Or they may, if
they can, escape abroad.

We who belong in the category of democratic
states have gradually developed certain basic premises regarding the nature and conditions of civili-
zation. We have agreed on certain terms for describing these premises, and we have invented
instruments for giving them effect and means for
changing those instruments if it seems desirable
to do so. The accretion of acknowledged principle
and agreed terminology enables us to talk intelli-
gibly with each other about our various activities
regardless of whether our ideas as to policy happen
to coincide at all points, or at any point.

Thus we know more or less what we mean when

we talk to each other about art, law, sport, education, religion, philosophy or science. We can exchange ideas whether we are Christians or atheists, whether we like Gainsborough or Dali, whether or not we believe in mental telepathy, whether we have round heads or long ones, whether or not we happen to favor the recall of judges or a federal education system or labor injunctions. We can do this because we have gradually acquired a common vocabulary. Our minds can meet, even in disagreement, because the words we use have meanings accepted in advance.

But how are we to talk to people who say familiar words but mean something else?

How, specifically, are we to discuss art with people who say "art" and mean "propaganda," to whom music by Mendelssohn is not music, and poetry by Heine is not poetry, and a novel by Thomas Mann is unworthy, not because of any artistic deficiency but because of some extraneous fact wholly disassociated from all possible measures of beauty and satisfaction?

Of what earthly use to us, except as exposés of the dictatorial mentality, are newspapers which are spoon-fed and censored to the point where they become (as Dr. Goebbels puts it) "sharp instruments of policy" and ready to be played on "like a piano"? There is no music for us—nothing but noise and boredom—when the Italian press carries out Mussolini's promise "to play on every string, from violence to religion, from art to politics." Publication in an Italian, German or Russian newspaper of a chance word that could raise doubts regarding the infallibility of the régime sends author and editor alike to prison; and the same thing happens in several other countries. The result is a deadly uniformity. The same "facts" are put together with scissors and paste from the same mimeographed releases, played up or down according to instructions, and accompanied by the hortatory, cajoling or threatening comment ordered for that day by the *Artifex Maximus*—Count Ciano or Signor Alfieri, or Dr. Goebbels, or the Moscow press chief.[1] All of it is stereotyped, sycophantic, flat despite the shrillness, dull. Gone is the reputation of the German scientific journals formerly read in learned circles the world over. Dead and buried are the famous old Italian and German newspapers—*Corriere della Sera, Berliner Tageblatt, Frankfurter Zeitung*—purveyors of news and

---

[1] *Giustizia e Libertà* (an Italian émigré organ published at 21 rue Val-de-Grâce, Paris) occasionally procures and publishes the daily secret orders issued to the Fascist press by the Ministry of Propaganda. The list covering the period May 1, 1936, to July 7, 1936, appearing in the issue of July 17, 1936, indicates the scope of the Ministry's activity. The 86 orders issued in that period include injunctions against mention of the promulgation of a new constitution in Soviet Russia (better that the Italian people remain ignorant of a dictatorship's decision to provide a façade of representative government); against estimating how many soldier dead can be contained in the "Ossario" at Amba Alagi (that might reveal discrepancies between reported and actual casualties in the African campaign); against mention of unemployment in Italian Africa; against reporting discussions of the International Labor Office regarding conditions and hours of labor; against publishing articles or pictures tending to show the "fraternization" of Italians and Ethiopians or to exalt "racial hybridism" ("Assoluta e netta divisione fra la razza che domina e quella che é dominata"); against giving details of the successful strikes in France; etc., etc.

organs of opinion once entitled to mention among Europe's half-dozen greatest. Pale impostors carry their mastheads and continue to use their type. Some of the old writers are at their desks; but daily they must be racked by the choice, "Shall we conform or starve?" Only minds deprived of the factual basis for critical judgment would give the printed product of this system of monopoly and terror the name "newspapers." Neither Germany nor Italy speaks to us from these barren leaves. And is it really the authentic voice of the Russia of tomorrow which speaks in the accents dictated by the Kremlin?

What can we or our children expect to learn from an educational system which does not proceed towards exact truth by historical research, healthy skepticism, experimentation and free speculation, but (in the words of the German leader) aims to produce "the political soldier"?

Shall we go, as our fathers often did, to study science at German universities? They now demand what one of the most eminent of living scientists, Lord Rutherford, calls "that strangest of qualifications for the life of scholarship, 'Aryan' genealogies." Their classrooms and laboratories are closed to physicists like Albert Einstein or James Franck, physiologists like Gustav Hertz or Otto Meyerhof; and they would not now admit men like Ehrlich or Fritz Haber who were their glory in days past.

Shall we go there for morals? "Important is not who is right," said Dr. Goebbels, to whom every teacher, writer and artist must make obeisance, "but who wins." The moral degradation indicated by this remark is explicitly affirmed as the aim of German teaching in a publication of the "Deutscher Philologenverband" urging that youth be taught not to reverence moral force, "which belongs to bygone times," and not to bother about whether he is acting nobly or basely ("the thing that matters is that he *acts*"). Here is the objective he is to be given: "to will with cold blood the anarchy of the moral world." [2]

Shall we go there for art? Forget the void left by all the musical and theatrical artists who have been expelled from Germany or who refuse out of dignity and principle to perform there, and judge the state of German art from a single specimen statement made by the man who is its official curator, Dr. Alfred Rosenberg. The German farmhouse, he writes quite seriously, "was the prototype of all later architecture. The farmhouses of northern Central Europe were the inspiration and source of strength for those who later on called themselves Greek when they went to the Balkans. The German peasant house is the original model of the Grecian temples and still today is an eternal model of German and Nordic architecture." [3]

Shall we go there for historical research? "We will never approach history impartially, but as Germans," writes the Nazi educational organ, *Die*

---

[2] Quoted by Ernst Wiechert in a speech at the University of Munich, April 16, 1935.

[3] "Blut und Ehre," Munich, 1934, p. 187. The 1936 edition indicates that 70,000 copies of this work have been sold to date.

Deutsche Schule (September 1933). But it was Dr. Rust, Minister of Education, who most authoritatively revealed the Nazi method of research in his address to the scholars gathered to celebrate Heidelberg's 550th anniversary. He emphasized Nazi emancipation from "the false idea of objectivity," and announced that "the old idea of science based on the sovereign right of abstract intellectual activity has gone forever." Symbolically, the statue of Athena, goddess of wisdom, had already been removed from before one of the great college buildings (given by American friends of Heidelberg, many of them of Jewish descent), and replaced by the German eagle; and above the portal the inscription "To the Living Spirit" had been blotted out and replaced by the words "To the German Spirit." Obedient to Dr. Rust's admonition, German scholarship the next day buried its dead with these fateful words of Dr. Ernst Krieck, Professor of Philosophy at Heidelberg: "We do not know of or recognize truth for truth's sake or science for science's sake." [4]

---

[4] The *Frankfurter Zeitung* of June 30 and July 1, 1936, and the *New York Times* of the same dates, after reporting the speeches of Dr. Rust and Professor Krieck, gave the names of six American citizens who accepted honorary degrees from Heidelberg at the same ceremonies where those speeches were pronounced: Reginald A. Daly, Professor of Geology at Harvard; William May Garland, realtor, of Los Angeles, Cal.; Henry K. Janssen, manufacturer, of Reading, Pa.; Kirsopp Lake, Professor of Ecclesiastical History at Harvard; Dr. Harry Hamilton Laughlin, biologist and eugenist, of the Carnegie Institution; and Ferdinand Thun, manufacturer, of Reading, Pa. How different were the speeches made three months later at Harvard's Tercentenary, and what another glory in consequence belonged to the honorary degrees there conferred.

What do we find if we turn to contemporary intellectual and artistic life in Italy for inspiration and instruction? Let Signor Paolo Orano, Member of Parliament and Professor of the History of Journalism at the University of Perugia, define for us the duties of the present-day Italian teacher: "For Fascism such things do not exist as a philosophy independent of race; a culture without a nation; a world without an empire; knowledge which has no end but itself, a limbo for those who are afraid to devote themselves to proselytizing . . . All without exception must bear their part in the policy of Fascism, in private and in public, in every lecture room, from every pulpit. Woe to those who teach the youth of today that there is a culture which 'takes no interest in politics.' " No wonder that where such requirements prevail one renowned scholar after another has preferred retirement or exile—De Sanctis, foremost authority on Roman history; Salvemini, foremost historian of the Risorgimento; Venturi, foremost historian of art; De Viti de Marco, author of classic works on finance; and a long list of others. Croce meanwhile writes in parables or is silent, Ferrero has escaped to Switzerland, and Sforza expounds the philosophy of politics in every language but Italian. The gaps thus left will not be filled by the uniformed professors of philosophy and history and science that I saw in Rome, wheeling up and down, gun on shoulder, outside the Mostra della Rivoluzione Fascista, executing the tours of duty necessary to prove their ability to teach the majesty of matter over mind. Nor is the blank that is Fascist art rendered less conspicuous by Fascist Italy's boycott of Toscanini, whose pure and soaring spirit bars him automatically from consideration among the fit inheritors of the tradition of Dante.[5]

Ortega y Gasset has written in "The Revolt of the Masses" that the Fascist and Syndicalist ideologies have introduced to modern Europe a type of man who does not want to give his reasons for his beliefs, or even to be right, but simply to have the power to impose his opinions. "This is the new thing," says the Spanish philosopher, "the right to be unreasonable, the 'reason of unreason.' " Doubtless there are men who would like to teach the truth as they know it at Bonn and Heidelberg (whence Spinoza could not now receive the invitation sent him early in the period which we call "modern times" to come there and enjoy "the utmost freedom of philosophizing"), at Bologna and Padua (where Galileo's inquiring mind would find itself in trouble today fully as much as it did in the seventeenth century). But the reason of unreason has them in its vise. From none of them can those who are not in that vise learn anything except a mortal fear of being similarly caught.

[5] To Toscanini the weekly review *Libro e Moschetto*, which interests itself in the cultural education of university students, offers not homage but this: "I spit in his eye." (*Cf.* "Italian Intellectuals Under Fascism," Student League for Industrial Democracy, New York, p. 12.) The Italian press was of course silent about New York's demonstration of admiration for Toscanini when he made his farewell appearance with the Philharmonic-Symphony Society; but it printed columns about the various performances of a black-shirt band which made a propaganda tour of the United States.

How are we to compete in games with people to whom sport is meaningless except as a channel for propaganda, at home and abroad, and as preparation for war? One of the clearest avowals of the dictator's conception of sport as propaganda was contained in dispatches from Berlin dated January 8, 1936, quoting as follows a prominent Nazi official, Dr. Kurt Muensch: "The non-political, so-called neutral athlete is unthinkable." Those who are "politically blind," he added, cannot be allowed to be victors, because "victors must be pioneers in political influence." Which is to say that the word "sport" does not mean a game as we mean it, either amateur or professional, but a political weapon. It operates to attract and regiment the young by allowing only those who conform to make use of sporting facilities or to be "victors;" and it advertises successes in international contests as triumphs of the "new race," the "new state," the "new social concept," over old and effete races, states, systems.

The second business of sport is to condition young men physically and psychologically for service to the régime. Senator Maraviglia, member of the Fascist Grand Council, writes: "Sport is not an end in itself . . . By popularizing and militarizing sports, Fascism accomplishes its greatest governmental work." [6] The ultimate service demanded is obviously death on the field of battle. Dictators do not conceive of war as a dire possibility which may be forced upon them, but as an instrument of

[6] *Cf.* John R. Tunis, "The Dictators Discover Sport," *Foreign Affairs*, July 1936.

policy which may be useful at a given moment to
the party-state. Because their ultimate reliance is
on force they must always speak of war as en-
nobling for those who participate, as something
desirable in itself.[7] And because the chief ally of
those who plan offensive war is the ignorance and
pride of their subject masses they must inculcate in
the young such a disdain for knowledge and self-
criticism that all individual doubts will be drowned
out in the universal roar of approval when the
loudspeakers carry to every corner the leader's ex-
hortation to attack.

Mussolini simply blurts out his inner conviction,
then, when he says that peace is "absurd." He considers that peace is *not* absurd only when he perceives nothing which can be won by war, or by
the threat of war and at the risk of war. Hitler has
admitted the same thing at least as often as he has
said the contrary. The contradiction is only in
terms. When he says that he does not intend to
start a war he means that when the moment comes
for rearmed Germany to take what she wants, the
responsibility for any war which ensues will lie not
with him but with whoever opposes. Everlasting
peace, he writes in "Mein Kampf," would doom
mankind to destruction. He believes that when
confronted with tremendous battles for self-pres-

[7] Generals sometimes have a different idea. Thus Marshal Ba-
doglio on June 6, 1936, gave an interview in which he said that
war is a horrible thing, to be deprecated as such (*New York
Times,* June 7, 1936). The next day Mussolini failed to appear at
Badoglio's triumphal review. On June 11 came the news that
Badoglio had resigned as Viceroy of Ethiopia.

ervation, "so-called humanitarianism, that product of a mixture of stupidity, cowardice and superciliousness, will melt away like snow in the March sunshine" (p. 148). He often interjects pleas for peace, but they are as terrifying as his threats, for it is to be a peace "established by the victorious sword of a master-nation which leads the world to serve a higher culture" (p. 438). And again: "Indeed, the pacifist-humane idea may be quite good after the most superior persons have conquered and subdued the world in such a measure as makes them its exclusive master . . . Therefore, first fight, and then, perhaps, pacifism" (p. 315). And again: "Anyone who really from his heart desires the victory of the pacifist idea in this world should support by every means the conquest of the world by the Germans" (p. 315).[8]

Germans, echoes General Goering, are proud to be known as militarists; and as justification he cites the fact that Prussianism is no longer a geographical but an ethical conception. Von Papen struggles to keep in Nazi good graces by proving that the Potsdam

---

[8] The first edition of "Mein Kampf" appeared in Munich in two volumes, published respectively in 1925 and 1927. The last page of the second volume contains the statement that it was written in November 1926. The Duchess of Atholl has pointed out in her leaflet, "Germany's Foreign Policy," that this was more than two years after German reparations had been reduced under the Dawes Plan and more than a year after the Locarno Treaties had guaranteed Germany against aggression. All the quotations given in these pages are from the edition of 1936. They appeared in practically identical phraseology in the original edition. Incidentally, all except the third of the quotations printed above are omitted entirely from the version of "Mein Kampf" published in America as "My Battle."

of today, far from having shed its traditional character, now goes Hohenzollern militarism one better; Germany, he says, has finally dropped the word pacifism from its dictionary; the new Germans must be "physically and morally warriors," dreaming of the opportunity that may be vouchsafed them to die in battle rather than ignominiously in their beds.

The means for making these visions come true are the schools and the youth organizations—in Germany the "Jungvolk" and "Hitler Jugend," in Italy the "Figli della Lupa," the "Balilla" and the "Avanguardisti." Soviet Russia has parallel organizations called the "Octobrists," the "Pioneers" and the "Komsomol." The child is put on the right track as soon as he can salute and play at soldiering.[9] The schools direct [10] and limit [11] his mind;

---

[9] Describing an exhibition of Italian toys held at Turin, the *Gazetta del Popolo* (June 25, 1936) writes that it "shows many new and original products, such as . . . machine guns mounted on tricycles, little armored cars instead of ordinary toy automobiles, and much other war material which is not expensive but gives much amusement." (*Giustizia e Libertà*, July 17, 1936.)

[10] Even subjects like mathematics and chemistry are harnessed up. The German secondary schools now use textbooks with titles like "Mathematics and Defense Athletics," with problems in gunnery, topography, etc., and "School Experiments in the Chemistry of War Materials," dealing chiefly with poison gases. The London *Observer* (July 5, 1936) gives an example from one of the new school arithmetics: "Bombing aëroplanes, flying during the day, go at a speed of 280 kilometers an hour. Night bombing aëroplanes can only fly at 240 kilometers an hour. How many hours will each class of bombing aëroplanes need to cover the area between Breslau and Prague, Munich and Strassburg, Kiel and Metz?"

[11] "The race-bound national soul is the measure of all our thoughts, aspirations of will and deeds, the final criterion of our values." Dr. Alfred Rosenberg, "Der Mythus des 20. Jahrhunderts," p. 697.

and the youth organizations through which he successively passes harden his body in route marches, gunnery and bayonet practice, gas drills and field maneuvers. Then, ignorant of the world and feeling it his enemy, strong in determination and in body, he puts on the colored shirt of the Storm Troopers or Fascist Militia or the tunic of the Reichswehr or Red Army. It is hard to think of any part of the program as "sport." The twelve-year-old boys I saw one Sunday morning near the Wannsee, gathered in trenches, and solemnly throwing dummy hand grenades at each other, seemed very far away from baseball on the back lot, hockey on the village pond, even from that thin upper crust of spectacular American sport which is publicized and promoted for cash.

How can we discuss legal rights and wrongs with people to whom "law" is party expediency or personal whim? Reichsminister Frank, sweeping aside the civilized conception that what is not prohibited is allowed, writes that when no specific law applies the Courts shall mete out punishment "according to the underlying idea of the penal code or according to healthy public sentiment." "Whose idea?" asks Professor McIlwain.[12] And whose sentiment? Answer is given in the decision of the Labor Court at Weimar published February 14, 1936, and reported the next day in the *New York Herald Tribune*. A group of "Aryan" workmen employed in a certain enterprise demanded the discharge of

---

[12] C. H. McIlwain, "Government by Law," *Foreign Affairs*, January 1936.

a Jewish fellow employee for fear they might be contaminated by associating with him. This Jewish workman, who was married, had served at the front in the World War and had been several times wounded; his factory record had no blemish. In upholding the discharge, the Court admitted that it could point to no specific law to support its decision, but found the necessary authority in the "legal instinct" and "legal feelings" of the Nazi Party.

The "model laws" which certain American professors acclaim after spending a summer in Soviet Russia would be challenged by those same professors as a return to barbarism if they were proposed in the United States. A theft of state or collective property is punishable by death; wives and children may be seized as hostages for the good behavior of husbands and fathers, and may be banished to Siberia for crimes they know nothing about; political prisoners have been executed without public trial, without public accusation or notice, and without benefit of counsel; "class enemies" are sent off to peonage in remote regions or put at forced labor in chain gangs.[13] The word "law" as uttered and applied in Soviet Russia is separated from the same word as used in the travel books of American professors by all that has happened in penology from the Middle Ages to this day.

Deutsche Justiz, publication of the German Ministry of Justice, puts concisely the disdain that any dictator must feel for legal systems: "A handful of

---

[13] "Paradise Imagined," by William Henry Chamberlin, *American Mercury*, September 1936.

force is better than a sackful of justice." This organ
of German law only echoes Kim: "A good stick is
a good reason." What respect can we feel for the
word "justice" if under its cover a dictator can define crimes after they have been committed and
mete out punishments as he is moved by whim or
expediency? What meaning can we find for it when
it covers jail and physical abuse, without charge
and without trial, whether at Oranienburg, or at
Narym, or on the Lipari Islands?

Some sort of religious belief, whether or not it
finds expression in any organized way, is common
to very many of us. What if "religion" means something hard and exclusive, something that makes
one cocky and ruthless, something to be withheld
rather than shared? What basis for communion is
there with people who claim to be Christians but
who exclude fellow-Christians with Jewish blood
in their veins from coming into their churches?
Interchange of ideas ceases with a man who can
write as does Professor Arno Schmieder: "The
Nordic lives in God. He feels himself to be God.
In his feeling and his will he is God himself." Or
with a man like Dr. Alfred Rosenberg, official Nazi
Leader for Culture, who propagates the degraded
superstition that the race to which Christ belonged
is a "bacillus which poisons our blood and our
souls." [14] Frank persecution and proscription of

---

[14] "Die Deutsche Schule in Deutschen Staat," by Arno Schmieder, Leipsig, 1935, p. 7; and "Blut und Ehre," by Alfred Rosenberg, Munich, 1934, p. 112. Dr. Rosenberg's mind was once described by Hitler as the only one in the Nazi Party which he
really respected.

any and every form of religion—even by such people
as the late Lunacharsky who elegantly compared it
to "a syphilitic disease"—is somehow less cheap and
offensive than a phenomenon like the German Faith
Movement and spoilt-child statements like those of
one of its leaders, Ernst Bergmann: "We cannot
kneel down before a God who pays more attention
to the French than to us!"

What meeting of minds can there be with scientists who think that the word "Aryan" is a race
term? Who think that there is such a thing as race
purity? Who think that there is such a thing as
fixed race superiority? Who despise and mistrust
the pure sciences and favor applied science, and
yet who are so mystical that they teach that practical discoveries in chemistry or medicine made by
non-Aryans should be ignored because they must
be devices to degrade superior peoples? Take a
single statement by one of the pseudo-scientists
whose works can be published in Nazi Germany
though Einstein's cannot: "Hereditary cancer is
the conflict of races within the human body." [15]
Could Pasteur engage in profitable discussion with
a man who says that? No more than regimented
scientists could in a million years come to understand those diffident and tentative processes by
which Darwin developed his origin of species theory, as revealed in a casual sentence which he wrote
to a friend in 1844: "At last gleams of light have

---

[15] "Neue Grundlagen der Rassenforschung," by Hermann
Gauch, Leipsig, 1933, p. 74.

come, and I am almost convinced (quite contrary to the opinion I started with) that species are not (it is like confessing a murder) immutable." [16]

The profound difference between true and spurious scientists, of course, is that they face in opposite directions. A scholar imbued with cold scientific zeal, aiming after knowledge and truth for their own sake, builds out his chain of knowledge and invention and discovery, link by link, into the void of the unknown. He is indifferent where the chain of reasoning and fact is going to lead him so long as he can satisfy himself that the links are sound. But the dictator forbids that sort of adventure. He forbids curiosity. He faces the scientist the other way about, assigns him his conclusion in advance, and tells him to work backwards from it by inventing supporting theories and neglecting discordant facts. "We do not know of or recognize truth for truth's sake or science for science's sake."

In those distant worlds slogans flourish. The first Secretary-General of the Fascist Party, Michele Bianchi, remarked that "without a special rhetoric it is not possible to make a revolution." A new patter must be invented; old evils must be rendered more palatable by calling them by new names. Thus the "corporation" is devised in order to coat with new procedures and new terminology the bitter fact that both worker and employer have been put into a straitjacket, that freedom of employment no longer exists, and that labor's hard-won

---

[16] "Life and Letters of Charles Darwin," I, p. 384.

right to collective bargaining through freely chosen representatives has been abolished. The "Stakhanov plan" tries to popularize the "speed up" and the "stretch out." [17] Words like "coöperation" and "unification" conceal the dispossession of racial or political minorities and the transference of their belongings to the party faithful. In our terminology "revolution" means a violent uprising of extragovernmental groups against the government; a "coup d'état" means an act of violence by which those in power get rid of their opponents regardless of law; and "terror" means violence carried on with the connivance or participation of the legal authorities. In Fascist terminology the coups d'état of Mussolini and Hitler and the terrors by which they suppress opposition are called "revolution." Events no longer flow from causes; it is the effect which is called the cause. When the Italian Government attacks Haile Selassie it reviles him for "provocatively" withdrawing his troops into the interior; and when the League tries to lend the Emperor its promised aid, Rome calls that action "aggression." Fascists label anyone who is not a Fascist a "Communist," though that person may detest Communism quite as much as Fascism: some mud always sticks. And the Communists label as "Fascists" even old Bolsheviks who abuse Stalin for letting world revolution lag. Both invent euphe-

---

[17] Not always successfully. A dispatch to the *New York Times,* dated Moscow, March 3, 1936, said that the Soviet press had just reported the second case within a fortnight in which an ambitious pace-setter had been killed by his enraged fellow workers.

mistic phrases to describe the instruments of their terror: already "protective custody" and "state-encouraged colonization" and "transported for reasons of health" are well established on the list of older alibis headed by the familiar "shot while trying to escape."

Fittingly enough, these revisions in the vocabulary are carried out not by the traditional tyrant and his praetorian guard, but by a "leader" aided by a pretended "élite." And if an appearance of ratification seems for some reason desirable, it is secured not by an election but by a "plebiscite" in which there is only one ticket and only one possible vote—"yes." With the elimination of the word "no," and the substitution for it of the word "yes," which thereupon assumes the duty of expressing both approval and disapproval, the dictated reform of the dictionary reaches its logical and ultimate conclusion.

Even the past is called back. Fact succumbs to fable. By the rules of the new Nazi history a man who volunteered and died for his country is no longer a hero if his mother or his wife who mourned him was a Jew. His name is no longer allowed to figure even on the list of soldier dead. "We do not know of or recognize truth for truth's sake . . ." Can we conceive of Washington or Lincoln trying to build greatness on a lie and robbing a dead man of his honor? We come here to such a divergence from the ideal of what seems to us an honorable patriotism that we find it impossible to follow further even in our minds.

Library
I.U.P.
ndiana, Pa.

321.4   Ar57w

c. 1

THE GULF BETWEEN

A great gulf indeed is fixed between the two conceptions of life. Nor does there seem a way to bridge it with words, because on the two sides words no longer have any commonly accepted meaning.

III.

WHO, WHOM?

At bottom, no type of mind is so like the extreme Right as the extreme Left.

—*Albert Pauphilet* (1915)

THE dilemma I have been attempting to expose by the "case method" is of course an old one in history. But never has it seemed so fatally presented as in our world of great industrialized nations, bound together by the intricacies of modern finance and commerce and forced into more and more intimate contact by the progress of science. A closely guarded frontier is no protection against shouted radio propaganda; the sky above any European capital can suddenly be darkened by aëroplanes which have set out without warning from hostile territory only an hour or so earlier; germs and poison gases can destroy masses of civilians if one man in a foreign state fancies to give the order. In the dictator's home realm, science furnishes him with as many tongues as there are pairs of ears to listen, and once he has won his way to power it makes him almost impregnable. No ancient or medieval despot could harness the opinion of his subjects and switch it about as he can; he knows that provided he is alert and decisive it can have no existence apart from his will, that he can shoot down even his comrades with impunity provided he himself edits the story. He is accountable to nobody for his expenditures. Particularly in his dealings with other governments does he feel that no hand but his own is on the brakes. Diplomatists and army chiefs can counsel caution; but they gape with admiration when he disregards their advice and hands them victories they would not have dared try for. His actions can be, and are, capricious, ruthless and (in the short view at any rate) stunningly effective. No sudden opportunity to levy international blackmail, appropriate somebody else's property, cow a rival or beat an enemy need pass unexploited merely because of the existence of an informed and articulate public which has qualms of conscience or doubts whether the achievement would be worth the risk.

Public opinion in a democracy becomes excited all too easily over fancied wrongs and neglects only too often to make allowance for the differing needs and habits of other peoples. It may respond to base appeals in a rush of anger, and it may be victimized by demagogues. Free discussion often degenerates into polemics. But provided the relevant facts are public property, and provided divergent opinions regarding them can be thrashed out openly, the possibility always exists that in the course of time differing interests will somehow be accommodated.

Relations between nations, after all, are not unlike relations between individuals. The fact that two human beings living near each other are literate and adult does not necessarily mean that they become fast friends. But the possibility of friendship is there. So with nations; they may become friends provided they are not childishly impatient and egotistical, provided their interests are compatible and their ideals civilized, and provided popular feelings on either side are not deliberately excited or warped for selfish ends by a régime which is able to control news and regiment opinion. And just as real friends are tolerant of each other's foibles, so nations that come to develop a feeling of friendship as a result of normal and frank intercourse build up a cushion of understanding that is very useful in breaking the first shocks of dismay and anger in a moment of crisis.

But what are we to think of the international friendships manufactured with scissors and paste in press bureaus and plastered across the front pages of controlled newspapers and chanted over controlled radios? People in a country under a dictator wake up any morning to learn that a certain other country, perhaps one that never was particularly esteemed, has overnight become wholly admirable for artificial reasons best known to the Minister of Propaganda; and shortly afterwards they may very well learn, again overnight and again for occult reasons, that that same nation is now to be considered despicable and dangerous and deserving of extermination. Of what worth is a friendship procured in these circumstances? The dictator may instruct his press to write exuberantly friendly articles about a foreign nation—but only so long as he receives a *quid pro quo*. Each time he cashes a check he makes ready to demand a new payment, and if it is not forthcoming the collaboration which the day before was made to appear the manifest destiny of two noble and kindred spirits will as easily be made to appear an anachronism.

In other words, international friendship, difficult enough to achieve between free peoples, and precariously maintained, becomes the hollowest sort of sham when on one side it is imposed from above as part of a dictator's system of diplomatic maneuver and blackmail.

No wonder that statesmen in democracies, who are accustomed to taking their political lives in their hands each day they hold responsible office, feel baffled when they face an antagonist who is able of his own single volition to stake the very existence of his race and nation—none daring to criticize or able to hinder—on some desperate gamble that feeds his vanity or promises to carry his régime through some hidden internal crisis. No wonder their rejoinders to such virtuosity, such magnificently reckless frivolity, seem cautious and niggling and inhibited. In a thousand ways the modern dictator is more formidable than the "man on horseback" with whom their predecessors had to cope. He is mounted on swifter steeds and possesses more sudden and wholesale means of attack than were dreamed of by Attila or Napoleon or even von Kluck or von Mackensen. He is simultaneously the man in the aëroplane, the man in the tank, the man in the submarine, the man behind the gas waves, the man at the microphone.

In no important instance in these last years has the effort to curb him succeeded. Not since Mussolini was balked in his Corfu adventure in 1923 has a ruthless militaristic government suffered direct defeat at the hands of the world community. The League and the United States could do nothing effective to prevent the Japanese war machine from overrunning northern China. Hitler's attempt to annex Austria at the time Dollfuss was murdered did not succeed, but this was due only to the unexpected clumsiness of the Austrian Nazis and to the fact that the German dictatorship had not yet come to terms with the dictatorship south of the Alps; the League did not determine the event, for neither Hitler nor anybody else believed that Great Britain and France were ready to use force to support the Covenant. Attempts by the League first to restrain Mussolini from attacking Ethiopia and then to punish him for his aggression ended in humiliating defeat. Encouraged thereby, Hitler threw the Locarno treaties into the dustheap, quite sure that there would be no effective reply either from the nations directly affected or from the League, into the framework of which the treaties had been carefully fitted. Little by little all pretense has been abandoned of maintaining the League administration of the Free City of Danzig and of giving its citizens international protection against Nazi *Gleichschaltung*.

The most recent scene of Fascist aggressiveness

has been Spain. The facts are vividly in our minds
—that is, unless we have happened to be readers
of the Hearst, Rothermere or similar papers which
labeled the legally elected constitutional government of the Spanish Republic as "Reds" and "Communists" even in the first weeks when it contained
no Communist or even Socialist members, and
which hailed the army officers who had turned on
that government, sworn though they were to support and defend it, as "nationalists" or "legion-
aries" or "patriots" or "Christian nationalists"
(although Moors were doing most of the fighting).
News of the rising in Morocco reached foreign
countries on July 19, 1936. The Italian aëroplanes
which within a week were heading towards General Franco's headquarters at Ceuta had formed
part of the regular Italian armed forces up until
the very next day, i.e. until July 20 (as was ascer-
tained when several of them fell in French territory), and were manned by Italian army pilots
conveniently placed on the reserve list at the same
time. Tanks and other war munitions also began
going clandestinely to the rebels through Portugal,
whose miniature dictator naturally opened his arms
to every agency promising to spread Fascism
through the world and so to fortify his personal
position. Meanwhile the German battleship
"Deutschland" and the destroyer "Luchs" hastened
to Ceuta and amid welcoming rebel salvos de-
barked an Admiral and his staff to pay a call on
General Franco. With Moors in the forefront of
the rebel advance, supported by Italian and Ger-

man planes manned by Italian and German pilots, an American journalist returned from Spain with the impression that what was in course there was less a civil war than a struggle by a half-armed defense militia to repel a well-organized foreign invasion.

While the Fascist Powers were thus setting out to establish a Fascist ring around republican France the democratic governments were doing what they could to minimize the risks of a general war by attempting to draw a ring of neutrality about both Spanish factions. Premier Blum knew very well that a rebel victory in Spain meant that France would have a third frontier to defend; but he knew also that to sell arms to the Spanish Government (though clearly legal under international law) would soon bring France into direct conflict with the Italian and German Governments which were giving aid to the rebels (clearly illegally under international law), and that a European war might result. Would Great Britain join France both in demanding that Fascist aid to the Spanish rebels stop and in selling the Spanish Government the arms which it needed to defend itself? She would not. The best that Premier Blum could do, then, was to suggest that the arms-producing nations withhold arms from either side. Rome, Berlin and Lisbon gave the idea reluctant lip service; but by the testimony of reliable foreign correspondents on the spot they continued to supply the rebels. After long delays caused by the presentation of a list of Italian and German provisos which constitutional governments could not accept (that there be a universal ban on collections for the Spanish Red Cross, that expressions even of "moral solidarity" be suppressed, etc.), a diplomatic conference assembled in London to map a program for maintaining neutrality. The Fascist states bullied it into discussing nothing but questions of procedure. Arms shipments to the rebels continued. In retaliation, Soviet supplies began arriving for the Government, which by now had been pushed far to the left in its desperate effort to form as wide a front as possible against its foes; but they were meagre and did not decisively increase the Government's ability to resist. Labeled as "Red," exchanging atrocity for atrocity in a bloody chaos, it was left to its fate. The blackmailers had won again.

Such are the events which have given us notice of the aggressiveness of Fascism, of the affinity which Fascist dictators feel with each other and with reaction in every land, of the effectiveness of the colossal war machines which they have developed, and of their ability to blackmail nations which care so much about peace that they "settle" rather than fight. Dictators may from time to time coöperate formally with each other, despite professional jealousy; doubtless they hope to do so often in the future; but the fact is that their coöperation need not be explicit in order for both sides to profit— the mere fact of the existence of other dictatorial régimes gives each a delightful opportunity for free diplomatic maneuver, threat and extortion.

Can any nation on the face of the earth, wherever situated, however strong, pretend to itself that it is not affected by the rapid development of this portentous phenomenon? Is it not plain by now to everyone who bothers to think that the present masters of dictatorial technique enjoy overwhelming advantages as against the spokesmen of peoples who simply wish to continue living their own lives, in their own lands, under governments more or less of their own choice, and who have not yet begun acting on the realization that in order to fulfill that modest wish (for such they erroneously consider it) they must strengthen their powers of defense proportionately as their antagonists have strengthened their forces of attack? If history had not already furnished enough proofs, does not the experience of these recent years prove the untruth of the old truism that it takes two to make a fight?

It takes two to make an agreement; it takes only one to make a war. Now to embark on what is called a "preventive war" is practically impossible for democratically organized modern states (as France proved by remaining quiet in the face of German rearmament, when Germany reoccupied the demilitarized Rhineland, and while Fascist protégés of Rome and Berlin were being installed in Spain). The decision between peace and war, then, does not really rest with the pacifically inclined, with those who are willing to make great concessions to secure peace. It rests with those who wait only for circumstances in which they can make war successfully. And always there are important forces driving these forward, counselling them to seek new victories, to take new risks. One such force is the pressure of internal troubles, social or economic, which may make a foreign diversion desirable. Another contributing element is the fact that a dictatorship must always feel itself in danger so long as democratic states continue to be its neighbors, reminding its people in many ways, no matter how stringent the censorship, that there still is in the world such a thing as freedom. Without the great last victory over every stronghold of the intransigent liberal spirit—the spirit which holds that the price would still be too high even if an autocrat government were able to produce all the material rewards which it promises—the dictator cannot consider any of his other victories safe or complete.

The dictators know this perfectly well, and they have made their declaration of war in plain terms.

Hitler writes in "Mein Kampf" (p. 148): "Either the world will be governed by the ideology of modern democracy, in which case every issue will be decided in favor of the numerically stronger races; or it will be ruled by the laws of force, when the peoples of brutal determination, not those that show self-restraint, will triumph."

Mussolini announced in October 1930: "The struggle between two worlds can permit no compromise. . . . Either we or they! Either their ideas or ours! Either our state or theirs!"

Each showed he knew the law of survival expressed in the old Bolshevik query, "Who, whom?" —who shall destroy whom? Lenin put the application of that law to the Communist case in specific terms when he said that "the existence of the Soviet Republic side by side with the imperialist states for any length of time is inconceivable" ("Works," Vol. XVI, p. 102), and that "an obituary will be sung either over the death of world capitalism or the death of the Soviet Republic" ("Works," Vol. XVII, p. 398).

If we accept the struggle in the sense here conceived—as a struggle, that is, between two broad conceptions of organized life, under one of which men seek progressive emancipation from authority and privilege, while under the other they relinquish freedom of thought and enterprise to an omnipotent state—then we are not much impressed by the claim made by the Communist and Fascist dictators that they aim at opposite goals. In practice they are of the same world; both seek to atrophy the thinking function in human beings; the tools of oppression used by each are the same; and we whose form of government must logically be obnoxious to both may doubt whether the eventual paramountcy of one would be very different from that of the other so far as we are concerned.

For the time being, Lenin's projected universal proletarian dictatorship is not being aggressively fostered. Now perhaps it is true, as some think, that the Russian leaders, wholly engrossed with the task of establishing an equalitarian system throughout their own vast territories, are progressively losing their integrity and crusading fervor, and that as they turn to state socialism and as the new bureaucracy entrenches itself in power they will be able to dispense with the most brutal of their current dictatorial methods. Or perhaps they are deliberately recalling the missionaries of their political religion from the foreign field (and executing those at home who object), in order to attract democratic countries to their support in defending Russian nationalism against German and Japanese nationalism. Or perhaps, since the theory of Communism is arrived at by a process of reasoning—correct or fallacious—and not, like Fascism, compounded of unreason and mysticism, they are able to prescribe a tactical pause, to rest on their oars, sure that the greed and obstinacy of capitalism are working so effectively for world revolution that there is no need for supplementary propaganda. Or perhaps after all Stalin has been diverted only temporarily from his wider aims, and perhaps after purging away personal rivals he will create a more unified and efficient direction than ever for conducting revolutionary agitation abroad. These matters are still obscure, and each theory has something to recommend it. At least we are entitled to wait until the new "Soviet democracy" has been transferred from paper to practice, and until we have been able to examine that practice with a coldly critical eye, before we accept Louis Fischer's claim (*The Nation*, New York, August 22, 1936) that in presenting the text of a new Soviet Constitution, approved in draft form by the Central Executive Committee of the U.S.S.R. on June 11, 1936, "the dictatorship yields to democ-

racy" and that this is an event unique in history—
"the voluntary abdication of a dictatorship."

While we wait, "men from Missouri who must
be shown," to see the meaning of these and other
obscure developments in the Soviet Union, we may
continue questioning whether the lot of American
liberals and the fate of the institutions they think
important would be very different under a proletarian dictatorship from their situation under one that
stemmed from Father Coughlin or the Reverend
Gerald Smith or William Randolph Hearst or the
Black Legion or reactionary associations of manu-
facturers or backward-looking professional patriots or any of the other individuals or organizations, naïve or malicious, which alone or together
hold the seeds of a full-bloom American Fascist
movement. Gentlemen of easy faith like Sir Oswald
Mosley or Jacques Doriot can pass unscathed from
one tyrant's army to another's. Only the liberal is
sure to be killed if either triumphs. Of that much
we can be certain after watching the current dictatorships in action, whether they announce themselves as "of the Proletariat" or "of the Roman
Empire" or "of the German Folk."

In each case alike an allegedly superior man,
aided by what he calls an intellectual élite, ban-
ishes or kills every independent dissident and
imposes his private will on the masses for their
alleged benefit. In each case the interests of the
leader are rationalized into identity with those of
the party; those of the party into identity with
those of the state; those of the state into identity

with those of the nation; those of the nation into identity with those of the masses. So simple is the process by which the interests of the Communist or Fascist leader and the masses are identified! All intermediaries are swept away. No longer is it even "the state" which is "I." "I" now presume to be the people themselves—their voice (for they cannot speak), their ears (for they must not hear), their mind (for to think is forbidden them). In the Communist case, "I" work for the economic liberation of the masses—and the first thing that happens when a man is given a job in the Soviet Union is that his identity papers are impounded by the government official in charge. In the Fascist case, "I" work for the racial and national and psychological liberation of the masses—and the procedure adopted is to dope the public conscience, debase the public intellect, hide the truth, and excite popular passions to demand new outlets and new conquests, which will end either in a victory that enslaves other peoples and sharpens new appetites for new aggression, or a defeat that provokes national disintegration and a more desperate psychosis than ever.

"I am yours," the dictators say to their people, "and you are mine!" But is it an exchange of equivalents? Not for you and me, free Americans, accustomed to thinking and speaking for ourselves. We turn our backs on the mirage of an infallible government that knows how to give us work today and security tomorrow if only we will accord it blind obedience, and on the "God-controlled dictator" recommended by the Reverend Frank Buchman to solve our "every last bewildering problem." [1] Torquemada said he was God's instrument; and he solved the last bewildering problem of many a poor wretch by consigning his charred or racked body to the grave.

But actually it is not of decisive importance in this discussion to know whether or not the Kremlin has had a change of heart or objective or merely of strategy. In no case does the system of life called "liberal" lack determined enemies. The differences revealed in the first chapter between it and the authoritarian system, whatever its particular stripe and whatever its current degree of virulence, are profound and varied enough to be considered irreconcilable. Fatally, it seems, each conception must aim to eliminate the other from the face of the earth.

In this struggle we need all the strength we can muster. We would be naïve to think that we can fight the enemies of democracy with one hand, or that they will be either willing or able to leave us alone while we examine the state of our forces and leisurely discuss whether we need to strengthen our defenses by giving a broader and sounder base to our society of supposedly free and equal individuals. Nor is it the moment to examine nuances in program and rate one dictator as less obnoxious than another. No one who finds excuses for Musso-

---

[1] See the interview with Dr. Buchman in the *World-Telegram,* New York, August 26, 1936, and the editorial in that paper the day following.

lini's suppression of liberty in Italy can object to Hitler's abuse of intellectuals, pacifists and "non-Aryans" in Germany (as should be understood in time by some well-to-do Jews who when they view the Italian scene favor authority and discipline whatever the cost, and become indignant liberals only when they read about the excesses of Rosenberg and Streicher). No one who condones forced labor and abuse in Siberian lumber camps for peasants and others with incorrigible "individualistic tendencies" is morally entitled to attack Hitler for his concentration camps (though American anti-Fascists often seem able to make the distinction). Nor can we afford to accept as allies those who really are intent on forwarding some particular national interest but who from motives of expediency urge it as a collective interest of all freedom-loving states; the two interests are not necessarily antagonistic, but neither do they necessarily coincide (as might be more gracefully realized by Noble Lords who are capable of frightful indignation over Mussolini's disrespect for treaties in the neighborhood of the Suez Canal but who take no interest whatever in collective action to prevent the mailed fist from striking along the Danube).

The balance of world forces is not still. We have no grounds for believing that time necessarily works in our favor. Recently, indeed, the opposite has been the case. 1935 proved a catastrophic year for France. At the end of Laval's ministry she had only wounds to count—her alliance with England strained to the breaking point; the League system on which she formerly had centered her policy disrupted; her East European and Balkan allies disgusted, full of a sense of betrayal and fear, wondering how best to come to terms with the growing German colossus; and Italy, to placate whom Laval had vainly sacrificed so much, coming back continually with fresh demands for "payments on account." If 1935 was France's *annus terribilis,* half of the next year sufficed to show that now Great Britain's turn was come. The spring of 1936 was not over before British statesmanship had been forced to acknowledge the severest defeat since that suffered at the hands of Napoleon. Its ungrateful task became to pass off as best it could the undeniable fact that a great assault had been made with impunity on British power, prestige and honor. On top of these terrifying and humiliating events came the Spanish rebellion, encouraged and aided by the great Fascist states and their little middleman, Portugal, and carrying the threat that France would soon have a new frontier to defend and England be squeezed still further out of the Mediterranean and perhaps face a German base on the Cape of Good Hope route to India.

To underline these somber developments is not to prophesy that France is now doomed to take second or third place in Europe, that the days of the British Empire's solidity and greatness are at last numbered, or that constitutional government and the survival of the free spirit are to be despaired of in either of these traditional strongholds. But neither are we entitled to assume offhand that the dictators who believe these things—who pin their hopes on them and chart their policies by them—are wrong. It might be a wholesome exercise for isolationist sections of the American public to muse on the chances for the eventual survival of American democracy in a world where either France or Great Britain had abandoned its traditional form of government or had been forced to abdicate its freedom of action under menace of a foreign dictator.

It has already been suggested that instead of retiring to some corner when his bag of tricks begins to empty, the dictator will always prefer to take great risks in order to create a diversion—even the risk of perishing spectacularly in a general holocaust that would mask the failure of his régime.

If ever the delicate seismographs at the propaganda ministry record that the people begin to yawn in the propaganda movies or are nodding over the propaganda papers in the cafés; if the vast demonstrations of popular enthusiasm begin to betray too clearly what is the truth, namely that they have been rehearsed by a Dr. Goebbels or a Count Ciano; above all, if ever a film of discontent appears on the flashing eye with which the young generation is expected to greet the leader's appeal to work and march and suffer today for the rewards of some glorious tomorrow—then is the classic moment for him to make a new gesture, slay a new scapegoat, perform a new miracle, take a new risk. These are the moments when he has inspirations, walks in his sleep, shoots his friends

43

in their beds, makes his enemies viceroys or air marshals or special ambassadors, reiterates his devotion to peace, launches warships, has birthdays, plows fields to prove that he knows the dignity of labor, shatters microphones, lowers the age for little boys to start rifle practice and for little girls to drill with gas masks. These are the moments when no risk seems too great if it diverts public attention from delays in the scheduled arrival of the millennium—not even the risk of a general war. They are the moments for which nations that care about peace and liberty must be on their watch and in anticipation of which they must collect their strength, both moral and physical, both in collaboration with other like-minded peoples and by economic and social reform at home and by instilling as much efficiency into democratic processes of government as they can absorb and still remain democratic in essence and in effect.

IV.

MOBILIZATION

And we are here as on a darkling plain
Swept with confused alarms of struggle and flight,
Where ignorant armies clash by night.
—Matthew Arnold

THE answer to the threats of the dictators is not a "preventive war," nor is it a crusade to help one of the dictatorial ideologies conquer another. We should collaborate with all of them on routine matters in a fair spirit, keep every engagement entered into with them to the letter, and show calmness and official reserve in the face of provocative gestures so long as they remain gestures only. But we should be under no illusions that a live-and-let-live relationship between democracies and dictatorships can last indefinitely.

To recognize this does not imply a desire for war. Nobody who cares about the future of democracy wants war. The liberal states could fight, might win. But could their liberalism survive the wartime curbs that would be prerequisite to victory and the new waves of economic deterioration and social disorder that afterwards would overtake the victor along with the vanquished? Hardly. We must hope, then, that the final test will be post-

45

poned. We must turn every respite to advantage, learning from the past errors of others how not to behave in a crisis of representative government, and neglecting no opportunity of mitigating the economic and financial diseases which have persuaded great and proud peoples to accept as normal the mental and moral status of serfdom. Meanwhile the hour for one of the dictators may strike. Though they talk from Olympus they are not immortal. Always they run the risk that as with the hypnotized wretch in Thomas Mann's "Mario and the Magician" one of their subjects may suddenly retrieve his power of choice and turn in reckless passion on his tormentor. Or dog may eat dog; Nazi Germany and Soviet Russia may have it out over Czechoslovakia and the Ukraine, or Nazi Germany and Fascist Italy over Austria, or Japan and Soviet Russia over Manchuria. Any struggle of that sort would be ferocious, and before it was over the infallible leader on each side would probably have lost his aura and would be on the way to losing his crown.

The call is not for an attack on the dictators but for a general mobilization against all their conceptions and practices; for an increase in the sense of interdependence between free peoples; and for energetic efforts at home to broaden the social and economic bases that sustain a solid political union.

Thus it would be taking only the most elementary of precautions if in all international negotiations the statesmen who represent democracies

always started out with the determination to minimize minor conflicts between themselves, remembering how much it is in the interest of every
democracy that every other democracy be strong
and prosperous enough to maintain its existing
form of government. Naval and military discussions are obvious occasions where a full realization
of this common interest would often operate to
prevent a weakening of the sum total of liberal
forces in the world. Trade matters are perhaps
even more important. Tariff makers normally are
much more aware of domestic pressure groups than
of the intangible national interest that counsels
fair and considerate treatment of all nations, but
particularly of those likely to join in efforts to ban-
ish the embargoes, quotas and exchange restrictions
which have strangled world trade and retarded the
return of world prosperity. Of equally bad effect
are the restrictive and discriminatory measures
sometimes taken by nations possessing a monopoly
of essential raw materials (e.g. tin and rubber).
They can be the signal for bad-feeling and trade
conflicts between peoples which, if they understood their primary interest better, would on the
contrary be doing everything they could to stimu-
late trade between themselves and to increase the
general capacity of the world to consume. Sometimes, too, the financial Powers have manipulated
their currencies to suit their domestic convenience
without giving adequate warning to others and
ignoring the disastrous results which may overtake
precisely those nations which in the larger view

they should seek to strengthen and support; and sometimes they have held back from participating in promising plans for general currency stabilization unless their own internal price structure and trade promised to profit directly at the expense of somebody else. How much this sort of thing had become the rule was shown by the sigh of relief (not unmixed with surprise) that went up when the American and British Governments were able to join in lending encouragement and aid to Premier Blum in executing his painful decision to devalue the franc, an action hailed as presaging new prosperity and stability for the French Republic. The great democratic governments, if they are bold enough to work together, can evidently find many opportunities for administering the doses of freer and more trade and of money stabilization at home and abroad which are the antidotes to violent inflations and deflations, centralized economies, autarchy, and the concomitants of these—poverty, dictatorship, war.

Even sentimental manifestations of solidarity count. To those who sneer at "gestures" I repeat what the head of a young European government said to me a year or so ago: "I can't tell you what it means to despondent Europe when your statesmen speak proudly and confidently about the principles of democracy. We long to believe that the great citadel built by Washington and Jefferson still stands. But there is so much to discourage us close at hand that we are apt to accept as all too true the rumors that sometimes reach us about the power and stubbornness of the American opponents of social reform, about the effectiveness of the propaganda in favor of American autarchy, and about the cold indifference of many Americans to the fate of liberty in other lands. When your leaders reassure us that the old ideals still prevail in your vast territory, when they boast of democracy's ability to develop and endure both in America and abroad, they do for us all over again what Wilson did in 1918 when he helped us establish our independence."

But the liberal states have a more specific way of recognizing that all of them are engaged in a struggle to survive in their present form. They hold between them the world's purse strings. In rough figures, the United States as of August 1936 had 49 percent of the world's gold reserves; France, 16.5 percent; Great Britain, 9 percent; Belgium, Switzerland, Holland and the Scandinavian states, about 9 percent together: a total of four-fifths of the world's gold reserve holdings. Japan had about 2 percent, Italy about 1 percent, Germany practically none.

If the American bankers who helped finance Mussolini in the early days of Fascism appear now to have been a little naïve, they had the excuse at the time that the Italian dictator had not yet justified all the things that were being said against him. They still could brush aside allegations that he was a menace to international peace on the pretense that these emanated from party enemies or fanatics about personal freedom. "After all, his bark is worse than his bite . . . Haven't strikes

been stopped and don't trains run on time? . . .
Wasn't Matteotti a Socialist anyway? . . . What if
Italy does make loans to Albania at the same time
we make loans to her? It's enough for us that our
loans are covered . . ." And more of the same sort.
Now Mussolini's bark has been followed by his
bite. Japan has bitten, too, and Hitler's jaws are
open. But regardless of whether in the present
circumstances American bankers would still be
tempted to lend money to any of the dictatorial
régimes, the Johnson Act precludes them from
doing so in the case of any government which is in
default, or whose government agencies are in default, to the United States Government. They may
find loopholes for supplying revolving commercial
credits. But at least for the time being no formal
loans can be floated in this country for Fascist Italy
or Soviet Russia, nor for Nazi Germany which is in
default on sums due as a result of the war.[1]

But what about the European financial centers,
especially London and Paris?

The two great Fascist régimes are in financial
straits. They have been exhausting their gold re-

---

[1] It is hard to believe that even were there no bar a German
loan could really be marketed in the United States after the German Government had discriminated so flagrantly against American holders of Dawes Plan and other German bonds, and while
claiming that it had no exchange with which to pay interest on
its indebtedness, had nevertheless found funds to repatriate vast
quantities of its bonds at "fire-sale" prices. It is estimated that
long-term German bonds for which American investors originally
paid $400,000,000 have been bought back by Germany (profiting
by the low prices caused by her own default on interest) at a
cost of $160,000,000—a loss to Americans and a gain to Germany
of sixty percent.

serves and their stocks of raw materials in order to build up and maintain mighty fighting machines. The drafts on the future which they have been recklessly drawing are beginning to fall due. They cannot stave off payment forever. Will the governments or financiers of European democracies which are directly threatened by the growing strength of the two Fascist dictators now come to their aid with loans or credits? Will they, in return for verbal promises of future good behavior, ignore the record of aggressions already committed or attempted, ignore the grandiose promises which the dictators have used to whet German and Italian appetites, ignore the enormous resources accumulated by Berlin and Rome for launching surprise military attacks,[2] and save them from shipwreck on the only reefs which they cannot avoid by their own powers?

The members of the League exhorted Fascist Italy to abide by her solemn, specific and freely undertaken pledges. When she refused they enforced a schedule of partial sanctions against her, at great cost to themselves. Will they now agree to save her from the financial ruin occasioned by the very aggression they condemned? Having failed to restrain her by their half-hearted measures, will they try to buy her off from further misbehavior by providing her with money to exploit her conquests and arm

---

[2] Colonel Lindbergh, speaking at Berlin on July 23, 1936, said that the frightening progress of military aviation had abolished the time factor in defense and stripped nations of their armor.

for new ones? [3] True, Mussolini now says he is "satisfied." But so is a boa constrictor when it has just swallowed a calf. The intermission is only digestive.

And will either London or Paris assist Germany to pay for her colossal rearmament? Mr. Winston Churchill calculates that in the three years 1933–35 Germany's capital expenditure, almost exclusively for military preparations, totalled 10 billion dollars (London *Times,* April 24, 1936). Will London and Paris help her find part of this money? Will they help her increase the number of airplanes and guns and tanks which she counts on to overawe Austria, subdue Czechoslovakia, and execute other of the preliminary items on Hitler's announced program of expansion, thereby presenting the rest of Europe with the choice of promptly fighting the Germany they have just helped arm or of condoning her acquisition of fresh resources and man power wherewith to carry out new conquests? Prime Minister Baldwin has said that the Rhine is England's frontier. Even the London newspapers which are most con-

[3] Foreign capitalists still inclined to consider Fascism "conservative" please note that, following other confiscatory measures, the Italian Government recently decided to pay for the first part of its new "post-Ethiopian" armament by a forced loan. When the proceeds of this run out, where does it expect to find the rest of the 12,000,000,000 lire which it has begun to spend on new armaments? The Rome correspondent of the *New York Times,* who is careful never to speak out of turn, mentioned this sum in his dispatch of October 10, 1936, citing such details of the war preparations as 1,200 factories now engaged in work for the military ministries; contracts aggregating 140,000,000 lire just let for the construction of new military airports; ten new cruisers, two 35,-000 ton battleships and several ultra-fast cruisers in course of construction; etc., etc.

siderate of Germany do not suggest that England could afford to see her take possession of the Low Countries and the French channel coasts without a fight.

In the light of that fact, there would seem to be a message for England in the following passages from "Mein Kampf":

"There must be full and final clarity about one thing. The inexorably deadly enemy of the German people is and will be France." (p. 699.)

"The future objective of our foreign policy is not either East or West, but we must have an Eastern policy in the sense that this means the winning of needed land for our German people. As we need strength for this, and as France, the deadly enemy of our people, strangles us and robs us of our power, we must take upon ourselves any sacrifice which involves the destruction of French efforts to secure hegemony in Europe." (p. 757.)

"Only when Germany has fully realized this [the eternal conflict with France], so that the German nation's determination to live is no longer allowed to languish in mere passive defense, but is exerted in a definite and active policy and thrown into a last decisive fight with France, with the greatest of German aims at stake—only then will the eternal and unfruitful struggle between us and France be brought to a conclusion, but on condition that Germany looks upon the annihilation of France solely as a means of finally gaining the possibility of expansion for our people in another field." (p. 766.)

In private life wise counsellors advise against the payment of blackmail; immunity is not to be purchased, one payment leads to another. Public opinion in the democratic countries, and especially in England and France, must point out vigorously that the same rule holds true between nations. It must oppose any compromise or subterfuge, for whatever reason and under pressure of whatever threats, which will help save the Fascist and Nazi régimes from eventual bankruptcy and economic disintegration and confirm their liking for and reliance on international blackmail.

(A few words in parentheses to indicate why so many quotations from "Mein Kampf" appear in these pages. It has seemed worth while to quote so often from Chancellor Hitler's book because the international copyright laws have enabled him to deprive the English-speaking world of an opportunity of passing first-hand judgment on it. The 1936 edition carried the announcement that 2,470,-000 copies of it had already been sold or distributed in Germany. It is part of the curriculum in German schools and universities, the text of sermons, the inspiration of daily editorial comment. On Christmas 1935 German industrialists gave copies of it to all their employees. More recently, orders were issued to the civil authorities to present a copy as a *vade mecum* to each newly married couple (provided both parties were "Aryan"). The official organ of the Nazi party, the *Völkischer Beobachter,* describes it as the "Bible of the German People," containing "for the present and for the future the final principles of National Socialism." Yet this Bible which is influencing current world history so portentously is barred from all who do not read German, except in a mutilated form which gives anyone who bothers to compare it with the original the impression of having been devised less to enlighten the world about Hitler's ideas and policies than to persuade the world that these are different from what he actually states them to be when he addresses his own people in his own language.)

It would also be advantageous for liberal states to know as precisely as possible how other members of their group are going to act in a time of general crisis. False hopes must be shattered. Nations which need to be able to rely absolutely on each other's word must take care that their formal engagements correspond accurately with their prospective acts. Each may promise only a minimum of aid; whatever it is, the promise should be phrased so clearly that no misconceptions about it can occur. Attempts are being made to revise the League Covenant—either to eliminate its coercive provisions or to restrict responsibility for enforcing them according to some regional plan, or (the opposite course) to facilitate their automatic operation. In any case the aim is to particularize responsibilities, remove ambiguities and dissolve illusions. A similar obligation lies on the United States, which does not belong to the League and does not engage in the detailed negotiations at Geneva that clarify the position of member states in advance of any joint action.

To state elevated principles without elaborating the exact means by which they are to be maintained merely adds to the feeling of easy optimism which has kept many nations, the United States included, from recognizing that there are only two possible courses to adopt when a strong state prepares to attack a weaker one—to accept the aggression with a pretense of good grace; or to oppose it by preconcerted action between all nations which feel menaced by the growing tendency to recognize the *fait accompli* as a substitute for treaty observance and orderly negotiation. Any other course encourages the prospective victim to persist in hopeless opposition, leads to recriminations, weakens the attempt to build up an effective international organization, and ends by giving new kudos to the government which was ready to risk war with all the world, but which banked, successfully, on seeing the rest of the world back down. We were told a good deal at one time about the educational value of the Kellogg Pact. Since then we have been shown that under absolute governments which consider peace "ignominious" and liberty a "putrefying corpse" the only sort of education which can make headway is education not for peace but for war. A Kellogg Pact plays into such a government's hands. The dictator signs it with his tongue in his cheek, watches "internationalist" circles abroad succumb to its hypnotic and soporific properties, and then by contemptuously brushing it aside shows his subjects once again what a superman he is, how easily he masters effete governments that gabble about the "outlawry of war" and "moral sanctions." [4]

As for treaties, no one pretends that they are eternal. The Constitution and laws of the United States are not immutable; they have been, are being, and will be changed. But the change is made by agreed procedures. International treaties often set forth methods whereby they can be denounced or altered, and some provide for arbitration or adjudication in case one party feels that the agreement has been violated in letter or spirit. In the last five years there have been three occasions, already referred to briefly, when a Great Power, dissatisfied with its position in the world, has taken the law into its hands to break it. Each disdained the procedure which it had itself elaborated for settling questions of interpretation and enforcement, and faced the world with a *fait accompli*. Each revealed the tactical advantages which autocratic governments enjoy as against those which have to reckon with an informed and conscientious public opinion.

Japan in 1931–32 broke the treaties which she had signed at Washington ten years earlier. They had

---

[4] Some may argue that similar criticisms apply to the League Covenant. But, unlike the Kellogg Pact and vague engagements like the Rio de Janeiro Anti-War Treaty, the Covenant prescribes a definite procedure both of conciliation and enforcement. Even though this procedure is not followed successfully in a specific case, supporters of the League are entitled to hope that it can be improved and that a majority of states can be brought to observe it. But who is so extraordinarily optimistic as to think that a mere self-denying ordinance will be observed by a government which wants to make war and perceives an opportunity to do so with impunity?

brought her definite advantages, specifically a better strategic position as the result of undertakings by the United States and Great Britain not to fortify the Philippines and Hong Kong, as well as increased security from attack as a result of the limitation on naval construction agreed to by those two richer and stronger Powers. After making the most of these advantages, Japan repudiated the commitments which had formed her voluntary *quid pro quo.* Her troops overran north China, whose territorial integrity she had promised to respect. Incidentally (if that word is not too insulting), in addition to being a breach of the Washington Treaties Japan's attack on China was also a breach of the Covenant of the League of Nations and of the Kellogg Pact.

In face of Japan's ruthless resolution the other signatories of the Washington Treaties, the League Covenant and the Kellogg Pact faltered; and in the end they found no more positive means of reply to her aggression than to declare that they would not recognize its "legality."

Italy in the autumn of 1935 attacked Ethiopia, a state which she had herself helped bring into the League of Nations. The attack was in undisguised violation of the League Covenant, a document which she had herself helped draft. During the preceding months of open preparations she had ignored all attempts to turn her from her purpose, and she disdained to follow the procedures set forth in the Covenant which would have had the effect, if any just ground for complaint against

Ethiopia existed, of "legalizing" her direct action.[5] But to postpone the attack did not suit the domestic policies of Signor Mussolini, and would besides have wasted valuable fighting time. He offered no excuses for what he did; there were none to offer. As a result, on October 10, 1935, fifty-one governments joined in the verdict that "the Italian Government has resorted to war in disregard of its covenants under Article XII of the League's Covenant." Like Japan, Italy incidentally dishonored another of her signatures, that to the Kellogg Pact, and repudiated the Italo-Ethiopian treaty of August 2, 1928, providing for conciliation or arbitration of all disputes arising between the two countries. And when later the campaign threatened to drag on into the rainy season she shattered the remaining Ethiopian defenses by disregarding the treaty of June 17, 1925, ratified by Signor Mussolini's government on April 3, 1928, prohibiting the use of poisonous gases in war.[6]

---

[5] Paragraph I of Article XII reads as follows: "The Members of the League agree that, if there should arise between them any dispute likely to lead to a rupture, they will submit the matter either to arbitration or judicial settlement or to inquiry by the Council and they agree in no case to resort to war until three months after the award by the arbitrators or the judicial decision, or the report by the Council."

[6] A British Memorandum, issued at Geneva, April 8, 1936, listed the testimony of English, Norwegian, Swedish, Irish and International Red Cross doctors regarding their personal treatment of very large numbers of mustard gas burns among Ethiopian soldiers and civilians. Many of these and other doctors made statements to the press about the large-scale use of gas by Italian troops. Signor Gayda (*Giornale d'Italia*, April 8, 1936) suggested that the burns might have been self-inflicted, the result of Abyssinian attempts to use mustard gas against the Italians.

On May 9, 1936, Signor Mussolini proclaimed the annexation of Ethiopia; and on July 4, led by Great Britain and France, the League of Nations rescinded the sanctions it had imposed against Italy.

Germany, on March 7, 1936, sent her troops into the demilitarized Rhineland, violating thereby the Locarno Treaty which had been negotiated by Foreign Minister Stresemann, signed by him and Chancellor Luther (afterwards Chancellor Hitler's Ambassador in Washington), and accepted by President von Hindenburg. At the time the treaty was signed Germany considered it highly advantageous. It brought her a British guaranty against French attack, membership in the League of Nations, and an opportunity to contract the American loans which restored her economy and enabled her to rebuild her formidable industrial plant. Chancellor Hitler had announced that he considered the Locarno Treaty to be a binding obligation on Germany as recently as May 21, 1935—that is to say, only ten months before he proceeded to tear it up. He paid no attention to the obligation which each signatory assumed to settle any dispute regarding interpretation by legal procedure, though the French Government apprised him of its readiness to accept a judicial decision as to whether the Franco-Soviet Treaty of Mutual Assistance affected the Locarno undertaking adversely. The Locarno Powers (minus Germany, of course, and with Italy only present as an onlooker) met at London on March 12. France was unwilling to take the responsibility of dealing with Germany single-handed; and England was unwilling to act solidly with her. The French Government finally was persuaded that London should address a "questionnaire" to Berlin inquiring the terms on which the German Government would engage to respect the territorial *status quo* in Europe provided tacit approval were given the German reoccupation of the Rhineland.

No reply was received from Berlin. That was the end of Locarno.

In each of these three cases a Great Power refused to follow the procedure which it had agreed on in advance for terminating or modifying a contract no longer felt to be profitable. The juice of the orange had been sucked; the rinds were thrown contemptuously on the floor.

Now respect for treaties, as Walter Lippmann has pointed out, is not a foolish kind of punctilio which realistic persons do not have to take seriously. President Roosevelt merely said what is self-evident when he called it (January 17, 1933) "the cornerstone on which all relations between nations must rest." We can say without being pharisaical that what we have been witnessing is the destruction, at the hands of the Japanese, Italian and German Governments, of all belief in the truthfulness and honor of governments and hence of the mutual confidence which is the first requisite for any kind of negotiation, joint action or accommodation. It is a loss which cannot be accepted with equanimity. As between themselves, the liberal states which believe in the sanctity of voluntarily signed agreements should scrupulously observe such agreements; they should refine and clarify them so as to eliminate all possible grounds for reproach and recrimination; and, to prove that they are not disguising selfishness as respect for law, they should begin a conscientious study to determine: (a), how far the economic grievances of dissatisfied states may be considered real and legitimate; (b), how such grievances might be ameliorated without doing wrong to others; (c), how to make sure that concessions today did not simply lead to new demands and new threats tomorrow; and (d), how similar studies and successive adjustments might be conducted in the future without awaiting the prodding of new international crises.

Meanwhile, the mistrust we feel as a result of witnessing actual deeds of bad faith are not to be wiped away by verbal assertions of peaceable intentions for the future, the more so as the dictatorial régimes which we regard most apprehensively have put us on notice that they consider such assertions mere diplomatic finessing. Listen, for example, to General Constantin Hierl, one of Chancellor Hitler's closest confidants, head of the Labor Service, Secretary of State in the Labor Ministry: "There are two kinds of pacifism: true pacifism, which springs from a weak and sickly nature or from blindness, but which is honorably meant; and sham pacifism. This last is a political weapon and can serve for preparing for war. By putting the opponent to sleep with the help of pacifist declarations it seeks to induce him to neglect his armaments. The soporific fumes which it spreads over the enemy are useful to hide our own armament for war." [7] General Hierl's idea is not new. Fichte phrased it succinctly: "Promise peace, that you may begin war with advantage."

When Hitler protests his innate pacifism, then, he should not feel hurt if we refer him to his friend Hierl. When he says that his foreign policy aims really at peace, he must wait for us to believe him until he repudiates declarations like that of his Minister for Propaganda and Public Enlightenment, Dr. Joseph Goebbels: "The only instrument with which one can conduct foreign policy is alone and exclusively the sword." [8] And when he alleges that his vast rearmament is a gesture only for the moral satisfaction of German dignity he need not be surprised if we reply by quoting some words of his own uttered in 1930 when he was not yet in office and did not feel under any compulsion to dissimulate: "It is impossible to build up an army and give it a sense of worth if the object of its existence is not the preparation for war. Armies for the preservation of peace do not exist; they exist only for the triumphant execution of war." [9]

---

[7] "Grundlagen einer deutschen Wehrpolitik," National Socialist Library No. 12, 1929, p. 16. In an introduction, Gottfried Feder says that General Hierl's "programmatic declarations" must receive "constant diffusion in the widest circles."

[8] *Der Angriff,* May 28, 1931.

[9] Adolf Hitler in *Nationalsozialistischen Monatshefter,* No. 3, 1930.

We can draw no comfort from the assertion often heard that "95 percent of the people of the world want peace." In the first place, it probably isn't accurate; in many countries, small and big, a profound sense of injustice, a mistrust of all compromise, a feeling that any gamble is worth trying, have long prevailed far outside of government or army circles and have helped create the war psychology now pervading vast areas of the world. But even supposing it true that 95 percent of the 275,000,000 persons living in Italy, Germany and Soviet Russia instinctively prefer peace to war, the fact is without value or importance so long as the policies of those countries are determined not even by the other 5 percent of the population but by three individuals and three tiny groups of henchmen. I respect the ideal of collective security. But it is a delusion to imagine that a collective system can be established until the predominant opinion in the majority of the great nations really favors peace and until those nations are so organized governmentally that the longing can find expression in their day-by-day policies. The peoples that do want peace and that have governments responsive to their will must live somehow through the years between. To manage that is their problem.

V.

INSURANCE

The struggle for existence has been construed into the gospel of hate. The full conclusion to be drawn from a philosophy of evolution is fortunately of a more balanced character. Successful organisms modify their environment. Those organisms are successful which modify their environment so as to assist each other.
—*Alfred North Whitehead*

THERE are other and even more direct meanings for the United States in the rise of military dictatorships, the impairment of the treaty system, the collapse of the League's prestige, and the accumulating threat of a new European war.

Many Americans express indifference regarding the future relative strength of the various European nationalities. I can hear them inquiring what concern it is of theirs if the French take second or third place on the continent; or if the Poles or Czechs or some other "new" nation (new to those who never heard of John Sobieski, Kosciuszko or Paderewski, of Boleslav, Palacký or Masaryk) are again submerged in some greater national sea; or if exhausted Spain splits in pieces and loses to new expanding Powers the last remnants of her once unmatched empire; or if the Danes and Dutch bow before the Pan-German flood or the Swiss find their mountains no longer impregnable or the Baltic peoples again become doorsteps of Russia. Such things, they hold, are natural to Europe: mere reflexes of senseless old rivalries and conflicts, best forgotten or ignored in the wiser and safer New World. They shrug their shoulders, as though over something quite expected, when a government disregards treaties to which the United States is also a signatory, which maybe it initiated. They demonstrate to their own satisfaction that third parties have no legitimate complaint, and really are not affected, if the ancient Empire of Ethiopia is annexed by Italy, or if the Chinese of Manchuria have to begin paying taxes to Tokyo instead of tribute to a Chinese War Lord, or if the Balearics suddenly become an Italian base midway between Marseilles and Algiers. Some of them go so far as to feel certain that the United States would be able to remain aloof from actual hostilities even in the event of a general and prolonged foreign war.

In a surge of reaction against all that they had been through in 1917–1918 the American people decided to learn nothing from that experience. The war was over. Had we stumbled into it, idealistically perhaps, but needlessly? Or had we been inveigled into it? Millions and millions of Americans were told one thing or the other. They believed either quite naturally because both theories harmonized with the preaching of generations of patriotic orators to the effect that besides being invincible we are also the most tolerant and pacific of peoples. The natural isolationists found powerful recruits in 1919 as a result of chance—the chance that President Wilson neglected to undercut political opposition by taking a bi-partisan delegation with him to Paris, the chance later on that a physical breakdown kept him from seeing how necessary it was to satisfy certain sincere critics of the League Covenant in order to defeat the bitter-enders who from partisanship and personal hate had determined to wreck the whole new conception of international coöperation and security. But we must remember that the vindictiveness of Lodge, the political opportunism of other Senators, Hearst's anxiety to clean up his war record by touting a new hundred-percentism, and many other private projects, accorded perfectly with the nation's psychology at the moment—its reaction from great moral strain and terrific hullabaloo, its longing to get back to everyday life and to catch up with work put aside, its boredom with reading outlandish names in the papers and being told of its duty to races and causes it had never heard of before; in general, the spirit of "never again."

Jeers greeted anyone who asked in 1919 whether to say "never again," and really to mean it with all one's heart, was in itself enough. An apparently reasonable plan for making wars less likely was in one breath called a dangerous super-state and the next derided as an empty vision by the whole crowd of professional xenophobes and by every group with a grudge against some country which was to be a member of the new international organization. The League of Nations, they announced seriously, could "order out our boys" to die again in alien quarrels in far lands. Of course the unanimity rule governing League decisions provided that no single action could be taken at Geneva without the positive acquiescence of every member government. They ignored the fact. They also forgot that there had been no League in existence in 1914–1917 to "entangle" us in Europe's affairs or to "plot" to ship our boys overseas to win somebody else's war, but that we nevertheless had been irresistibly sucked in—despite patient efforts by a President whose heart was set on peace—because our government held to traditional rights which a foreign government calculated that it could disregard. I do not recall this here in order to indicate a belief that the premises adopted by the Wilson Administration in 1914 were necessarily correct, or that modifications in our traditional policy as a neutral might not mitigate the risks of our becoming involved in certain types of war in the future, but in order to underline the fact that neither in 1920 nor today have most "isolationists" faced realistically the doubt whether the American people would not again fight if during another protracted war between great nations a number of American citizens lost their lives on the high seas and the whole American economy collapsed as a result of belligerent interference with American commerce.

The plea to sabotage the League had a strong appeal—strong proportionately as the public was tired of responsibility and idealism. Many leaders of the campaign against it were too old to care or too ignorant to understand that the world had changed —still was changing—and with it the foreign problems even of the mightiest nations. They had no inkling, even after the Russian revolution and the toppling over of so many old thrones and powers, that a new era of social and economic experimentation was beginning, and that it was bound to color political procedures and the relationships of governments. It was nothing to them that the war had hurried science ahead to plow new channels of attack under the seas and through the air, to devise new and immensely deadly instruments for spreading death and destruction, and to catch all the peoples of the earth together in a new network of communications. So much of this would have been beyond their comprehension even if they had stopped to notice it. And they did not do so, any more than they noticed that the sapping of European financial and material resources and the stimulation of American production had reversed our former relationship to other countries, that we no longer were a debtor but a creditor nation, that now we must reorganize our foreign trade, import as well as export, and gradually revamp our domestic economy to protect our enormous new interests abroad and to maintain our standard of living at home. All this was beyond the comprehension of those who overrode the sober and experienced statesmen of both parties, smashed the proposal for American participation in the League (incidentally ending the League's hope of becoming a universal system), and gave the country the Harding-Cool-idge era and sky-high tariffs and a self-contained prosperity which was as specious as the comfortably restored sense of political isolation in which every-one again began basking. War? "Never again!" "Forget it!" "We're busy!"

Despite all the frenzy and confidence of the post-war era there still existed an American sense of idealism which felt frustrated and which kept on demanding that "something be done" to help stabilize world peace. But after the gleaming heights of Wilson's trajectory the plans with which surviving "internationalists" busied themselves seemed rather flat compromises with the isolationist viewpoint. As time went on they put their principal energies (apart from educational work about the activities of the League) into the agitation in favor of joining the World Court and the movement to "outlaw war." The Court is a highly valuable institution, though not likely in itself to prevent great wars; membership in it would not constitute a political entanglement or involve the compulsory submission of disputes involving vital national interests. Every President and Secretary of State since the Court was founded has urged that the United States join. But Congress has never agreed. The movement to outlaw war was more successful. It produced the Kellogg Pact, signed August 27, 1928, by fifteen governments and afterwards extended to include practically all the nations of the globe.

In the light of experience we are entitled to believe that the Kellogg Pact was a contribution less to world peace than to international mystification. And today we probably would be encouraging the nations to adopt a more realistic attitude toward aggression if we admitted that Japan and Italy had shown the Pact to be useless, and if (since we still are unwilling to help equip it with "teeth") we gave formal notice that no American riposte was to be expected to states which flagrantly violated it. We would, moreover, remove ourselves from a rather invidious position.[1] Similar considerations arise in connection with instruments like the Anti-War Treaty signed at Rio de Janeiro October 10, 1933, which in general terms commits its signatories not to recognize the fruits of aggression.[2] Does its generous phraseology imply obligations which we would hesitate to carry out in all circumstances? Can anyone conceive of its tangled provisions for *ad hoc* conciliation commissions being in the least effective in a serious crisis? If there is doubt on either point we probably would be acting in the interest of unambiguous international relations, and hence of peace, if we disassociated ourselves from the undertaking.

Not only should the United States avoid giving any impression of undertaking responsibilities

---

[1] See Haile Selassie's appeal to the United States in July, 1935, and Washington's reply (*New York Times*, July 5 and 6, 1935).

[2] Article II of the Covenant reads: "They declare that as between the High Contracting Parties, territorial questions must not be settled by violence, and that they will not recognize any territorial arrangement which is not obtained by pacific means, nor the validity of the occupation or acquisition of territories that may be brought about by force of arms." The United States ratified adherence June 27, 1934. Italy, incidentally, adhered March 14, 1934, though she did not ratify adherence.

which it will not execute; it should also refrain from saying it will not do things which it might do, and where possible it should make clear the things it definitely stands for and will uphold. If, for example, we can imagine conditions in which the American people would be stung into fighting for a cause less direct than the defense of their own shores, then we should not give anti-war pledges which might have the effect of encouraging other nations to take actions which would in fact precipitate us into war. If we have not yet found a comprehensive definition of our neutral rights which promises to withstand the strain of practical application in the event of a major war abroad, then we would be helping the cause of general peace as well as increasing the likelihood that we could ourselves escape becoming involved if we took great care that in relinquishing untenable or unessential "rights" we did not weaken any which in actual practice we might have to defend. If we are determined to maintain the principle of "America for the Americans" against any European or Asiatic attempt to acquire political power in the Western Hemisphere, then we should put the Monroe Doctrine on a multilateral basis [3] as

---

[3] In 1925 Secretary Hughes suggested a compromise between the view that the Monroe Doctrine should be multilaterally enforced and the view that we must continue to consider it as a unilateral declaration in order that we may act under it independently in case our interests are jeopardized by European or Asiatic imperialism. He proposed that each American republic announce the Monroe Doctrine as its own individual policy, safeguarding thereby the dignity and freedom of action of each state, yet giving the Doctrine a Pan-American sanction. (See Benjamin H. Williams, "American Diplomacy," p. 59.)

soon as possible and suggest to Canada that she associate herself with it on that basis.

Although the great 1920 argument over America's proper relationship to other nations still continues the isolationist viewpoint still prevails. Are there any indications of its being either more or less complacent and invincible than it was at the start?

Two of the great postwar crises revealed that although the United States Government had refused to join in the formal collective effort to protect international law and promote international security it nevertheless realized that those general objects concerned it directly. On both occasions the State Department tried *ad hoc* to harmonize its efforts with the procedure of other nations possessing similar interests and aims. Thus in February 1932 Secretary Stimson offered the British Government to proceed under the Nine Power Treaty in an effort to preserve Chinese territorial integrity, a problem with which the League Council was then vainly grappling; it was Sir John Simon who held back.[4] Again, in the autumn of 1935 Secretary Hull hastened to clear away possible American impediments to Geneva's projected action against Italy, only to find that Great Britain and France, the Powers chiefly responsible for League policy, had no real intention of making

---

[4] *Cf.* Henry L. Stimson: "The Far Eastern Crisis," New York, 1936, p. 162-164.

their threats effective.[5] The American Government's effort to throw its weight on the side of treaty enforcement failed in each case; but so far as the American public understood these efforts it apparently approved them. American opinion had at any rate become less blindly isolationist than it was in the days when the State Department was afraid even to acknowledge letters bearing the Geneva postmark.

The popular reaction to the Roosevelt Administration's course on the second occasion was particularly instructive. So long as the League gave an impression of sincerity and firmness (*i.e.*, before the Hoare-Laval proposals of December 9, 1935) there was every evidence that the American public, represented by "isolationist" as well as "internationalist" members of Congress, were ready to support the Roosevelt Administration energetically in requiring American exporters and shippers to avoid any activity which would put the United States in the position of interfering with or being involved in the League policy of sanctions. For once an American President found

---

[5] It would be interesting to know what information regarding British intentions Ambassador Bingham was sending to Secretary Hull during the period when the State Department was warning Americans not to travel on Italian ships, was cutting off the supply of arms and ammunition from both belligerents, and was appealing to American exporters to keep their trade with them at peacetime levels. And what information did the British Embassy in Washington give the British Foreign Office to justify Prime Minister Baldwin's statement on June 20, 1936, that it had been found impossible to impose oil sanctions for "the plain reason" that there were no grounds to suppose that the United States would refrain from supplying Italy with all the oil she needed?

something like agreement among the main groups of American opinion actively interested in avoiding war.[6] The *volte face* of Hoare and Laval put a stop to this harmony. And American chagrin over what was considered as Franco-British repudiation of the League (leaving the United States Government out on the limb) was not in the least assuaged when British public opinion forced Hoare into a humiliating resignation or, not long after, when Premier Laval also fell. The upshot was that Americans tended to draw back very far indeed into their shell. But until December 9 America was closer to Europe than at any time in fifteen years.

Apart from its action in the Manchurian and Ethiopian crises the principal occasions after the war when the American Government intervened in world affairs was when it took the lead in arranging a regional pact in the Pacific; when it unofficially sponsored efforts to wind up the reparations dispute; and when it became an active member of the Disarmament Conference. The Washington Conference was called to deal with difficulties in a part of the world where American "isolationists" are far less wary and touchy than they are in cases where European matters are under discussion; the limitations on American freedom of action in the Pacific agreed to in 1922

---

[6] See Dulles and Armstrong, "Can We Be Neutral?" p. 65-67, for the opinions expressed at that time by Senators Borah of Idaho, Nye of North Dakota, Vandenberg of Michigan, Thomas of Utah and Clark of Missouri.

by Secretary Hughes and his colleagues were accepted by the public as fully justified by the benefits promised in return. The reparations question involved material American interests, and American public opinion was proud of the rôle which American citizens played in settling it. Of disarmament, it probably is fair to say that Americans would have been willing for their government to join in any thoroughgoing plan of arms limitation; but there is no way of knowing whether they would have approved the plan for "consultation" offered by President Roosevelt through Norman H. Davis at Geneva on May 22, 1933, in the hope of facilitating a general accord. Big isolationist guns boomed promptly in the Senate when news of the Davis speech reached Washington.

Possibly the Senatorial investigation of war origins, despite (or because of) its amateurishness and its surprising dearth of surprises, will in time lead some younger political leaders to think out afresh the problem posed by the American determination to avoid war. May they reëxamine in a critical spirit, step by step, the American Government's actions from 1914 to 1917—free from presumptions that the national interest necessarily required fidelity to the traditional conception of "neutral rights," free also from the assumption of many current writers that American wartime leaders were legalists and pedants and the whole war generation moronic.[7] May they in the same way

[7] On this matter see Newton D. Baker, "Why We Went to War," New York, 1936.

reëxamine the decisions taken by Congress just after the war, unprejudiced by memory of the personal rivalries of those days of nervous exhaustion, of alternating lassitude and violence of spirit, and untouched by the lies, exaggerations and false logic which then so deeply affected public opinion. Incidentally, may they also learn the fallacy of the economic determinism that colors so much postwar talk and writing, and begin taking account of the power to sway men and nations which resides in abstract ideas and ideals. Only so will the generation now preparing itself to come to power be able to serve and protect American interests, long-range and general as well as short-range and specific, when proposals are made to nationalize the manufacture of arms or to accept obligatory arbitration in various categories of international disputes, or when they face questions as to the proper attitude for the United States to adopt toward a League which had become purely European, or one which, while aiming still to be universal, had shed all but its consultative and technical functions. Should we, in the first event, definitely waive neutral trading rights when insistence on them might bring us into conflict with a collective effort by European nations to suppress aggression? In the second case, would membership in a League without coercive power still seem to us a dangerous entanglement? Encouragement to expect the younger generation to show a realistic attitude toward questions like these is found in the new intellectual vigor and independence evident in the colleges. Nor is it a bad

sign that in addition to the attention formerly paid
to the legal and political aspects of international
relations there now is an increasing study of their
psychological and social bases.

Some useful result may also come eventually
from the almost religious campaign conducted to
force Congress to pass a law guaranteed "positively"
to preserve American neutrality in all future
foreign wars. As the great neutrality debate pro-
gressed the conviction must have dawned on all
open-minded persons, whether or not they had
ever given thought to such things before, that the
problem was not one which could be dealt with so
easily as first enthusiasts imagined. They began to
see that in any prolonged war between major
Powers (*i.e.* any involving real risks for the United
States), only a policy amounting to non-intercourse
with the belligerents could possibly succeed in
keeping us neutral. And they asked doubtfully
whether this policy might not involve such losses
for American trade and shipping, might not destroy the jobs of so many millions of farmers and
factory workers, that the Government soon would
be forced by public clamor to toss it aside.

Viewed in this light, the neutrality debate has
probably been a necessary stage in the education of
Americans toward a faint understanding of the
complexity of their foreign relationships and a
realization that their most elementary material interests—the day-by-day conditions of life on prairie
farms, in New England shoe factories, in Oklahoma
oil towns, in Oregon orchards, on Hoboken docks

—can be and are affected by the development and interplay of purely political forces in distant parts of the globe. We are not yet within sight of the time when the great American public will see that there is one way, and one only, for them to make certain of not being involved in future world wars: that there be none. But perhaps a dent in its complacency has been made. And of one thing we can be fairly sure. If ever there dawns the epochal conviction that America has a selfish interest in world peace, then the old political catchwords, though still printed in bold face in the yellow press and still shouted through the unoffending ether by all the priests frocked and unfrocked, will have a hard time keeping the American public from deciding that something practical ought to be done to get it. Americans are not fatalistic, nor are they uninterested in good trade, social quiet and everyday happiness. They simply have two discoveries still to make: that any constructive action of theirs in the international field can affect their everyday interests; and that it may be less dangerous to take that action than not.

Can we do anything to hurry the discovery along? We can continue to emphasize—as events continue to provide us with proofs—how fatally interrelated American prosperity and peace are with world prosperity and peace. We can identify and describe, again and again, the political forces both right and left which we think chiefly menace that prosperity and peace. We can applaud statesmen like Secretary Hull and Secretary Morgenthau who believe in taking the initiative, whenever the chance offers, in the only part of the international field where the American people at present sees the possibility of useful intervention—the economic and financial. We can fight every measure that would throw the United States into the ranks of nations which are trying to create their own separate autarchies by means of tariffs, embargoes, quotas and currency restrictions, with the result that trade is reduced to a barter basis, planned economies become tighter and tighter, national struggles for survival become fiercer and fiercer, and there are new incentives and excuses for war. And all the time we can urge the need of showing by the various means suggested in these pages, indirect and inadequate and unsatisfactory as they are, that the American nation is not oblivious of the moral antinomy which is splitting the world, not as some say into three camps—democratic, Communist, Fascist—and not as some say into two camps —Communist and Fascist—but into two more general yet distinct worlds, in one of which personal freedom still lives and in the other of which it is dead.

One's first instinct, told this unpleasant truth, is to think how to escape from the struggle. There is no escape, because the aggressive forces have acquired momentum which their leaders could not control even if they would, and because the battle front is world-wide. An American still may feel drawn for sentimental reasons toward this or that nationality, or he may dislike all foreigners alike, or he may care nothing about them one way or another. But nations are no longer divided from each other by nationality only, or by divergent economic interests, real or fancied. They are also divided as never before in modern times by the spiritual character of the social and political tenets which they profess and practice. Who even on this fortunate continent is so hardy as to think that his whole manner of life will not be directly affected, and that of his children's children after him, by the impending decision—What sort of government is to have the mastery of the Old World? Are human liberties now to be extinguished in the lands where they had birth?

Here, then, is a new factor to be considered and with it a new decision to be made. Which is more dangerous? To proceed on the belief that the apparently imminent trial of strength between the democratic and dictatorial philosophies of life will not in fact occur, and that even if it does the present internal structure and peaceful foreign relationships of the United States can continue unmarred by absolutism's triumph over most of the rest of the world's surface? Or to recognize that the test is only too likely to occur (many would say that it is already far advanced), that we care enormously about the upshot, and that we must be alert to favor in every way possible our friends and resist in every way possible our enemies?

The results of adopting the first theory are plain. So long as the world continues to be racked with uncertainty and insecurity we shall be helpless to bring about general and calm consideration of the problems of freer commercial intercourse and monetary stabilization. We shall be unable to face fairly the question whether it is possible to provide peaceful outlets for the energies of peoples which feel cramped and dissatisfied under present conditions. We shall continue to run the risk of eventually being implicated ourselves in wars which we might possibly have helped prevent. Moreover, we now know that wars, even for democracy, strain democracy to the breaking-point. A new force thus has been added to our hatred of war: we abhor it not only because it sucks our blood and wastes our substance, but because we have seen it endanger the political institutions in which we trust. Lastly, we shall have failed to do anything to encourage peoples placed today on the firing line of the old battle for human liberties. Searching desperately for new efficiency, new strength, may not some of these be tempted to sacrifice the very thing they wish to be strong enough to save? May they not throw overboard parliamentary procedures, the system of checks and balances between legislative and administrative authority, the ideal of applying the law as it is written and of changing it only by agreed legal means—in short, all those attributes of representative government which make it an awkward indeed guardian of liberty, but the only effective one known?

Then in a world weighted more heavily still against our conception of happiness and human dignity, and with a still more shrunken circle of states with which we can even pretend to have satisfactory relations, we would stand aghast at the consequences of having imagined that not to act is *per se* less risky than to act, that if decisions are continually postponed choices become unnecessary. To boast that we have no interest in the struggle for freedom is to encourage the forces that threaten it—probably to augment them—perhaps to make inevitable "the last battle of the west"—perhaps in the end to find ourselves fighting it alone. Of course it may not come to that. The spirit of liberty may be tough enough to hold its own on something like its present lines until of themselves the dictators tumble; or if they attack, it may repulse them without our help. How sure of this can we be? Facing the doubt honestly, is it not worth while to take out every form of international insurance which can be had at a specified and not too heavy cost, missing no practical means of supplementing the guarantee which is supplied by our own strength and our conscious determination to continue living a life of freedom?

VI.

THERE IS NO SOVEREIGN RIGHT
OF SUICIDE

The secret of liberty is courage.
—Pericles

AT HOME as well as abroad there is a front to be defined and defended.

To nineteenth century liberals the fight against tyranny was chiefly political. They fought for equal civil rights and for equal treatment before the law. We must struggle to keep their victory won, to see that groups and individuals do not feel driven to try direct action because legal action fails to secure them what the law says is theirs by right. Anyone who considers vigilance unnecessary might begin saying over to himself one by one the names of the several States of the Union. In how many cases the first thing the bare mention of a name calls to mind is not that State's honorable part in American history, or its notable resources or vaunted climate, but some long-continued and shameful legal discrimination or bare-faced abuse of justice.

But it is mainly in the economic domain that the old liberal fight now is continued and intensified. We shall have to use our best talents—urged on by a generous spirit, yet restrained by a perception of man's limited capacity for planning the endless details of his endlessly changing society—if we are to keep those who ask only a chance to make a living from being tempted or forced to invade the rights of others in the desperate search for work and security. An organized society which confesses itself unable to provide opportunities for work and open markets for doing business, which does not know how to prevent monopoly from fixing prices and debasing the standard of living, must admit a general failure according to any standards of efficiency or justice and is in a poor position to resist the pretensions of other systems.

These sound the merest platitudes. But they imply very much to anyone who thinks of liberalism not as an attitude of mind but as a positive and constantly developing program of action. We do not require to be assured that it is an infallible program; but we do need to feel that it is a hopeful and dynamic program, and that it opens up a tolerable course between two intolerable extremes—authority exercised without regard for the law as written and liberties exercised without regard for the interests of the majority. If we feel it does that, then we can defend it and fight for it, we can use all our strength against anyone who tries to operate outside our laws and anyone who thinks of overthrowing them by force in favor of something else.

The course of events in lands where representative government has succumbed shows that this is an expedient as well as an ethical attitude.

There was no living spirit of liberty in Russia under the Tsars and no opportunity to practise arriving at decisions by degrees, as a result of discussion and compromise. Government was by ukase. Opposition was revolution. The revolution of 1917 brought not liberty but chaos, and then a new tyranny in place of the old. Kerensky hesitated to push a thorough-going program of agrarian and labor reform and delayed in calling a constituent assembly. Weakness must have played a part in opening the road to power to men no more daring and ambitious than most of the Bolsheviks were when Lenin first arrived in Petrograd and began working to transform the revolution against Tsarist tyranny into a dictatorship of the proletariat. But probably Kerensky and his colleagues failed principally for the simple reason that they did not know how to establish the foundations of representative government and had no time to learn. Their failure to exploit their fleeting moment of power does not carry any very important lessons today for countries long schooled in the practice of liberty.

Unlike Lenin, the Italian and German dictators did not seize power in a period of chaotic change. They overthrew established constitutional governments and overawed constitutional chiefs of state whose sole excuse for being was to see that no such thing happened. How were they able to do this?

Obviously democracy in postwar Italy and Germany was not impregnable. It did not have behind it a long history of gradual development and success, and the problems of the period, both material and psychological, would have tested the popularity and solidity of any government. Both countries felt, though in different degree, the psychology of defeat and frustration. Germany had been starved, bled white, beaten on the field of battle and forced to accept a punitive peace. Later the Nazis rationalized the military defeat into a Socialist "stab in the back," blamed the Versailles Treaty on those who signed it rather than on those who willed and led the war that had the terms of that treaty as its epitaph, and then made these new myths the basis for an attack on "poltroon" and "traitorous" civilians, i.e. parliamentarians. The Italian people had been buoyed up during the war with promises of much property not conceivably theirs. When at Paris they did not receive the impossible which they expected they blamed the parliamentary régime for negligence and spinelessness, and accepted the thesis of "the mutilated victory."

But there were technical weaknesses in both parliamentary systems, and there were moral weaknesses in those who administered them. Both contributed to the gradual process of disintegration and to the ultimate overthrow. The number of parties in both countries was ridiculously large; there was much bargaining and maneuvering between place-holders; and political energies were continually being diverted into personal and party struggles instead of being applied to a serious study of the new economic and social problems. Coalitions were difficult to arrange between elements as divergent as the adherents of the Second International, those professing a liberal but not at all a Marxian point of view, and those under orders of the Catholic Church. And when coalitions were achieved they lacked unity of purpose and hence were without force and decisiveness. Such cabinets do not enjoy prestige. Nor did there appear at the right moment in either national arena a democratic statesman of the first calibre, determined to carry through a wide program of economic reform and renewal and to do it strictly within the framework of the constitution. As a result, the masses of the people gradually got the impression that by-and-large their elected representatives were not inventive and courageous enough to chart new courses to a more satisfactory national and international life. As for the constitutional heads of state, they simply did not have the capacity—either through physical infirmities or lack of principle or lack of stamina—to foresee the future or even to do their sworn duty at a given moment.

In Italy, the four years from the end of the war to the day Mussolini seized power from the feeble hands of Premier Facta saw no less than ten cabinets under five Prime Ministers; and in the last free elections, those of May 15, 1921, at least twenty parties and groups took the field. In Germany, between February 1919 and the day in January 1933 when President Hindenburg decided to bring the Papen-

Hitler combination into power, there were 21 cabinets headed by 12 Chancellors; and in the last really free elections, those of November 1932, 38 parties participated. The tendency for economic interests to determine political groupings made parties in both countries rigid, and rigidity tempted ambitious leaders to form "splinter parties" based on still further particularizations of class or group interests. But of more importance was the vogue for the system of proportional representation. This system did not operate to make small parties coalesce: each group thought that if it maintained its separate identity it might manage to secure enough votes to seat a few of its leaders. For example, in the elections to the Weimar Assembly in 1919, 29 party lists were presented and 10 of them secured representation; by the elections of September 1930 the number of parties presenting lists had become 37, of whom 16 secured seats.[1]

Both in Italy and Germany, then, the parliamentary system was distorted. Unusual boldness and singleness of purpose would have been required to make it function satisfactorily. Italian and German parliamentarians lacked those qualities. Moreover, they were too sophisticated to fear street-brawlers and demagogues, and too matter-of-fact to understand the power of uprushing longings and hates. They were paralyzed, finally, by a code of ethics that frowned on using force to reply to force.

---

[1] A. J. Zurcher, "The Experiment with Democracy in Central Europe," p. 86. See also Frederick L. Schuman's excellent volume, "The Nazi Dictatorship"; H. Kraus, "The Crisis of German Democracy"; and F. Ermath, "The New Germany."

In Italy, a succession of weak and undecided coalition cabinets prepared the way for an overturn. The Socialists consented too late to join a left coalition; by the time they made up their minds to it the Fascist coup d'état had already been planned, indeed the threat that the parliamentary paralysis would be overcome and that a strong coalition would set about restoring order in the country actually accelerated the execution of the plot. All through the time that the Fascist movement was gathering momentum the governing coalition lacked the participation of the Socialists, and often Don Sturzo's "Popolari" were in opposition also. The coalition cabinets governed largely through royal decrees (budgets were not even discussed in the Chamber), and maintained a "hands-off" attitude toward the open conflicts between armed Fascist bands and labor organizations which were of daily occurrence. They were worried that high army officers, police officials and even judges were involved in an illegal political action; but they did not know how to stop them. The final crisis of Italian constitutional government arrived in the last days of October 1922.[2] By then the habit of being lenient with everybody and of postponing hard decisions (which dated back to D'Annunzio's armed defiance of the government at Fiume) had become chronic. But there still was time to ward off the coup d'état by proclaiming martial law. On the morning of October 28 Premier Facta acquired stomach enough to ask royal assent to

---

[2] See G. Salvemini, "The March on Rome: Revised Version," *Current History*, October 1932.

such action; but the King, who at first seemed to favor taking a strong stand, had meanwhile got the impression that Facta simultaneously was negotiating with Mussolini, and he also had received warnings from Admiral Thaon di Revel, General Diaz and other military chiefs that they favored the Fascists and that the Duke of Aosta was on their side. After much hesitation the King finally decided to make terms with the groups gathering outside the gates of Rome. For this purpose he gave Salandra a mandate to form a Cabinet. After spending the night of October 28 in a fruitless negotiation with men much more determined than himself, Salandra threw up the task. Fascist bands meanwhile had poured unopposed into the city. On the evening of October 29 Mussolini left Milan, whence he had been observing events, and marched on Rome in a sleeping car, arriving there the morning of the thirtieth. King, Parliament and constitution were lost. They did not revive. A chance to retrieve the situation came later on when the Matteotti murder discredited Mussolini and gave him a moment of panic. But the "Aventine opposition" under Amendola waited for the King to give the lead; and the King waited for the encouragement of public opinion. As later on Baldwin waited for Haile Selassie to relieve him of the dangerous task of imposing effective sanctions, both waited in vain.

The German Republic's fifteen years of life tell a story different in detail and in tempo, but not dissimilar in its lessons. At Weimar the Social Democrats were dominant; they gave the Republic its first President. But even in the first days after the revolution against Kaiser, army and Junkerdom they did not seem to understand the brutal reality of the struggle on which they were embarked; they lacked faith in the inevitableness of their reform program and confidence in their ability to carry it out.

Now no revolution, as Dorothy Thompson says, ever was made by a syllogism. The German republicans worked hard; they overcame the Ruhr crisis; they secured the Locarno guarantees and membership in the League; they got loans abroad. But a desire to persuade the Allies of the need for new concessions always held them back from advertising their foreign successes to their own constituents. And the Social Democrats, that part of the governing coalition which had the program and duty of reshaping the German social fabric, failed to stake its existence on a struggle to break the monopolistic power of big industry and to execute the land reforms authorized in the Weimar Constitution. They spent much time in organizing their party representation in the Reichstag. But the governments in which they participated were usually found picking a delicate way around the great citadels of reaction that had been left intact in the army, the judiciary and the bureaucracy. Step by step they compromised with reaction, at first because they lacked courage to move ahead by themselves, later because they hoped to persuade conservatives to support them rather than the more violent Nazis. The Catholic Centrists, all along unsatisfactory allies, in the end proved disloyal to the republican régime which they were committed by oath to preserve. Dr. Brüning had already accustomed the German people to the idea of emergency decrees. Now he became earnestly persuaded that salvation could be found only through the establishment of a monarchy of the limited English type. Once he had started negotiations looking to that end and had admitted the fact to President Hindenburg he no longer possessed any real argument against those who wanted to go much further—particularly against the Nationalists, who, headed by von Papen, argued for the restoration of a Hohenzollern monarch even more frankly autocratic than William II had been. Actually the Nationalists were no better political realists than the Social Democrats and the Centrists. Urged by von Papen, President Hindenburg accepted an illegal government in violation of his oath to uphold the constitution. That was the end of the Nationalists; the Nazi fish swallowed the Nationalist fishermen. It was also the end of the Social Democrats and Centrists, who went *en masse* to jail, concentration camps, exile or the grave. Partners in the same fate, not inappropriately, were the German Communists who as part of the sterile tactics ordered by Moscow had often joined the Nationalist bloc in the Reichstag in opposing all economic and social reform, their hope being to provoke a general breakdown and new opportunities for the spread of communistic ideas.

This account of some of the moral and technical weaknesses of the Italian and German parliamen-

tary régimes is not meant to minimize the extent
to which they were dominated by their economic
environment. Pareto has pointed out that if governments are to keep in power by the very expensive modern art of government rather than by
using main force they have urgent need of economic prosperity. "To drive a despot's subjects to
revolt," he wrote in 1916 in "Mind and Society"
(IV, Par. 2305), "sufferings far more serious are
required than are required to cause a government
nowadays to lose an election." England was able
to surmount her ten-year depression without dam-
age to her civil liberties, French democracy sur-
vived rigorous deflation and two devaluations, and
both countries and the United States have so far
come through an unprecedentedly severe world-
wide economic crisis without political disaster and
without turning to leaders more revolutionary than
J. Ramsay MacDonald, Léon Blum and Franklin
D. Roosevelt. Their democratic foundations had
been well and deeply laid. But no such old foundations existed in Italy and Germany.

The rise of Fascism in Italy coincided with the
postwar depression and deflation. Progress was
made directly after the war in restoring Italian
finances and industry, but the end of 1921 and the
beginning of 1922 were a time of depression in
Italy as in many other countries, America included. Improvement began in the spring of 1922
(as noted in the reports of the American Commercial Attaché in Rome, and as confirmed later by
as important Fascists as G. Volpe and Giorgio Mor-

tara), but the beneficial effects of the upturn did not make themselves generally felt in time to counteract the Fascist appeal. In Germany, the increase in Nazi strength in the Reichstag came after the onset of the depression in 1929, and especially after Chancellor Brüning adopted his stringent deflationary policy of increased taxes, decreased salaries and decreased social expenditures in the summer of 1930. The National Socialist Party's 200,000 members in January 1930 had doubled by January 1931; and whereas only 12 Nazi deputies had been elected to the Reichstag in May 1928, 108 were elected in September 1930 and 230 in July 1932. The German people had not hung William II, von Hindenburg, von Tirpitz and von Ludendorff in 1918 for leading them to defeat. They had borne their wartime privations and the bitter misery that followed—wild inflation, lost savings, devaluation. They had begun again. But in 1929, when American loans ceased and the world economic crisis stifled business activity and a new period of hard times set in, then the Nazis were able to persuade this long-suffering people to place a heavier responsibility on the men who had tried to mitigate the consequences of the war—Ebert, Erzberger, Stresemann and the other statesmen of the Republic—than on the men who had chosen to have the war. Neither the pre-Fascist cabinets in Italy nor the pre-Nazi cabinets in Germany had the prosperity described by Pareto as necessary if they were to continue for long in office without having resort to semi-legal methods and in the end being compelled either to maintain themselves by force or to make way for those prepared to do so.

The rabble rousers who came loudly into the streets promised everything, stopped at nothing. They played on all the strings of patriotism and heroism, obscurantism and mysticism, hatred and envy. In Germany they aggravated the inferiority complex that had grown up as a result of the defeat and the Treaty of Versailles, and appealed to the nostalgia for old prestige, for the sense of "belonging" both in a disciplined domestic society and in the front rank of the Powers whose fit duty it was to order the destinies of the world. In Italy they reawoke the hopes and ambitions that had gone down in "the mutilated victory"; they sneered at the "old-fashioned" idea of Garibaldi and Mazzini that a people united and free and industrious possesses the means to be great and happy, and put in its place the picture of a new Roman Empire to be won by arms. They attacked the blatant profiteers of the German inflation, promised to reform hard and reactionary employers, inveighed against the "tyranny of interest." They promised the wandering and "disinherited" the jobs and possessions of the old bureaucracies and of racial and political minorities. They invented a myth and a ritual. They shouted invocations to the gods and heroes of Imperial Rome and the firelit halls of Valhalla. Siegfried the dragon killer lived once more, "thief smellers" again sought out scapegoats to satisfy the lust of outraged communities, Caesar mounted an armored car. To a scene that was drab and slack they gave back color and action and symbolism and nonsense. They had a passion to astound, and they astounded.

Their first converts were found among the restless and dissatisfied men of the war generation and their younger brothers; then they won over sections of the middle class whose savings had been wiped out and who envied the rigidity of labor wages; then they attracted everyone who thought he might get something for nothing if the promised scapegoats were really offered up on the pyres of class and racial hate; and then they took into camp the stupid and gullible leaders of big business and finance who decided that a governmental house-cleaning and some blood-letting in radical and labor ranks might be a good idea, who felt confident that afterwards the agents hired to carry out the work could quietly be put aside, and who imagined that the brittle dictatorial wall which separates the passions of Communism and Fascism would never be pierced in the shock of some national crisis nor corroded by a slow rebellion against the stubbornly reactionary grip of monopolistic industry and monopolistic capitalism.

To this aggregation of sentiments and passions the disjointed forces of liberalism, republicanism, socialism, pacifism and communism found no way of making answer. They did not in any sense form a united front. Sapped by defections from both wings, hampered frequently by the hesitancy and opportunism of their leaders, betrayed at last by

their rulers, the disciples of constitutional government yielded place, without even a final struggle,
to the coalition of frustration and hope, envy and
avarice, idealism and self-sacrifice, megalomania
and intrigue. Once shared, once yielded, power
was gone forever. Now it belonged to those who
dared exploit it without limit. Now Italian King,
German President, employer, employee, reactionary, radical, would-be neutral, all chanted "Duce!
Duce!" or shouted "Heil Hitler!" or learned to be
silent. Their individual wills and separate destinies disappeared irrevocably under the steam-
roller of the totalitarian state.

Such the precedents. They bring the sobering
realization that revolutions are less often won by
revolutionists than lost by their opponents. Strong
in that knowledge, we must hold tight to legal pre-
scriptions and procedures, trust only to leaders
committed by instinct and belief to the defense of
civil liberties, and deal summarily with those who
band together to destroy them. We must guard
zealously the rights of our scholars and teachers to
carry forward the stream of civilized thought; love
art for art's sake and honor science when it seeks
the truth; and encourage and protect the rights of
assembly and speech and the freedom of the press,
remembering what a wise Chinese philosopher
says, that "while the Fascists regard the press as a
nuisance and therefore suppress it, the believers
in democracy also regard the freedom of the press
as a nuisance and thank God they have so glorious

a nuisance." [3] It is our duty and interest, too, to examine with an open mind every proposal which has the aim of better adapting the technique of government to changing requirements of modern life. This mention of efficiency does not in any way imply that it is the chief measure of a government's virtue, as many persons seem to believe. The things a government does not do are often as much a virtue as the things it does. Certainly, however, efficiency is one of the measures. If representative government is *tolerably* efficient men will have one less temptation to throw their troubles on the shoulders of an infallible savior even at the cost of becoming chips on the ocean of his unbridled passion.

But all this is only part of the story. "Shame," cried Nietzsche, "on the ignoble happiness that is the dream of grocery clerks, Christians, cows, women, Englishmen and all democrats!" People who are happy, however, are not generally ashamed of it. People can be persuaded that happiness is somehow ignoble, that self-immolation is the natural lot of man, only when they are not happy and when they see no chance of happiness for themselves or their children. If we learn from the course of events in Germany and Italy we will urge our leaders (and then permit them!) to try to provide a better life for more people. They will not achieve this by attempting to plan the multifarious details of all the daily occupations of every citizen (deciding how many chickens are to be raised in order

---

[3] Lin Yutang, *Asia*, November 1936.

to lay an imaginary minimum quota of eggs, or charting the graph of future automobile production in accordance with changes in the birth rate),[4] by creating new state monopolies and by centralizing direction in a new state bureaucracy—but by rescinding the monopolies and privileges that already exist and by exacting that the concentration of wealth and business power in gigantic corporations free from the responsibilities and liabilities of the ordinary citizen shall not break the spirit and tie the hands of individual initiative.

Nor in emphasizing the necessity of change and adaptation are we going back on our past. It is a fundamental American belief that political control exercised directly by the people is, in spite of disappointments due to the inertia of the masses and the occasional ascendancy of demagogues, the surest guarantee against usurpations by a class or a group or an individual megalomaniac. This belief was put concisely by Thomas Jefferson when he said that "the evils flowing from the duperies of the people are less injurious than those from the egoism of their agents" ("Writings," IV, p. 23). Jefferson himself foresaw that adaptation would be inevitable. "We might as well require a man to wear still the coat which fitted him when a boy," he wrote, "as civilized society to remain ever under the regimen of their barbarous ancestors" ("Writings," IV,

---

[4] Would any state planner in 1920 have thought that the 8,225,859 automobiles then registered as being in use in the United States justified the creation of facilities for making the 22,565,347 in use in 1935?

p. 41). To say that a democracy of liberty-loving individuals must continuously be fitting itself to the requirements of a world constantly being made over by science and industry is not to impugn it, but to credit it with strength to support even a very heavy new burden.

Meanwhile, it would be disastrous to think that devotion to liberal standards requires us to remain on the defensive against those who frankly announce that if once they can manage to secure power they will kill the democratic system of government that gave them their chance. Fascists and Communists so proclaim, and have given proof that they mean it. We must let them state their aims and make their arguments. But remembering that their language never means what our dictionary would tell us it means, we must turn on it the devastating light of truth, never relaxing our vigilance simply because they use good words to cover bad deeds, never accepting their pretension that violence and injustice today are the path to peace and justice tomorrow. Truth, their mortal enemy, is our ally. It has made and it will keep us free. Above all, never must we let them organize their power. Our government's own legal armed forces are excluded from the making of policy. Pressure by armed groups of any description is intolerable; the mere existence of such groups constitutes pressure; they must never be allowed to organize. The right of assembly is not the right to wear uniforms and bear arms, freedom of speech and conscience does not mean the right to advocate the abolition of free speech and freedom of conscience. And always we must recall the precedents of Italy and Germany to those who might be tempted for selfish purposes to coöperate politically with demagogues and embryo dictators, counting on being able to use them for a time without letting them in the end get the upper hand.

Our fathers won their liberties by force, in three centuries of struggle. Programs of action to take those liberties away by force give notice that we must be ready at some point to reply in kind. To say that there is such a point is as compatible with true liberalism as self-defense is compatible with devotion to peace. "Are we only to be permitted to defend general principles," asked Lord Morley, "on condition that we draw no practical inferences from them?" No.

To be liberal does not mean to understand all principles and to have none. The democratic principle is that the majority has the right to govern and that the minority has the right to criticize and oppose the majority. The liberty of the majority is limited by the right of the minority to dissent from the majority; in this right originate all the other rights of the citizen. But the right of the minority to dissent is limited by the right of the majority to rule, and by the majority's duty to restrain minorities which threaten to overthrow the majority by force and destroy all liberties. The majority has the moral right to exercise power, but it is the trustee of that right and must so exercise its power that a different majority may overrule it tomorrow, and another majority may overrule that one the day after. The majority of today shall not put chains on itself and on all future majorities any more than it shall make people of a particular color slaves. It shall not accept a dictator. Even the sovereign right of the people stops short of the right of suicide.

This is not a compromise between doctrines. It is *a* doctrine, the democratic doctrine, which proclaims the right of free competition between political parties composed of free individuals as the best method of assuring peaceable progress. It proceeds through trial and error. It is based on the assumption that no man is infallible and that there does not exist a political science. When one discards this doctrine one must accept the dictatorial doctrine, according to which there are infallible men whose commands are not to be opposed. Lenin was right, Mussolini and Hitler are right: between the two doctrines there is no compromise. Our society or theirs. We or they.

INDEX OF NAMES

INDEX OF NAMES